IN PRAISE OF YOUNGER MEN

'How many women, approaching or in their forties, long to re-shape their destiny? To escape the routine of their lives, whether it be the domestic round, the daily commuting train or bus, or the dreariness of a meaningless social existence? ... To be people in their own right. And how many have the courage to do it, to accept the challenge when opportunity comes rapping on the door?

'This book is about sex, and life.
The older woman, sex, and life.

'It is about making the decision to enjoy the rest of life; the decision not to lament the past or waste time regretting mistakes made but rather to regard them as lessons learned for future benefit.'

Also by Sandy Fawkes
in Hamlyn Paperbacks

KILLING TIME

IN PRAISE OF YOUNGER MEN

SANDY FAWKES

Hamlyn Paperbacks

IN PRAISE OF YOUNGER MEN
isbn 0 600 36364 3

First published
in Great Britain 1979
by Hamlyn Paperbacks

Copyright © 1979 by Sandy Fawkes

The four lines from *Cabaret* on page 16
are reproduced by permission of
Carlin Music Corporation

Hamlyn Paperbacks are published by
The Hamlyn Publishing Group Ltd,
Astronaut House,
Feltham,
Middlesex, England

Set, printed and bound in Great Britain by
Cox and Wyman Ltd
Reading

To all young men in general
and to Barry in particular

CONTENTS

INTRODUCTION

I have to admit that there was a time when I had grandiose ideas (it was about six months ago, which just shows you learn more quickly as you get older) and I had intended to write a book that was going to be a definitive treatise on the changing status of the forties-plus woman in the Seventies and Eighties. There was also the thought that it could be one of those socially significant documents freeing women from the taboos of the past, offering them a new assessment of themselves in mid-life and a licence to enjoy the second halves of their lives more than the first.

What a pompous load of old bullshit that turned out to be!

This book is about sex, and life.

The older woman, sex, and life.

It is about making the decision to enjoy the rest of life; the decision not to lament the past or waste time regretting mistakes made but rather to regard them as lessons learned for future benefit.

I am not given to flowery statements as you will notice as you read further, but a woman in her forties can, and should, be as glorious as the countryside in late summer; succulent, ripe and burgeoned with riches. She has survived the frosts of May, weathered the rains and grown strong. She is alive – and should be proud of the fact, not ashamed because she is no longer a frail, questing shoot. She has reached the age where she can afford to be generous with love both to herself and others; it is the time of gratitude for the gift of life, her own private harvest festival.

I wish to assure you that it is pure selflessness on my part that makes me sit at home and tell you all this. I have a marvellous life and want you to join in the benefits. Why shouldn't you, too, wake up mornings with a hangover, think 'Oh, Christ, who's this?' or just 'Oh, God, what did I do?' Why shouldn't you, too, race to work with yesterday's mascara on, and desperately have to surround yourself with friends who will tell you that the night before you were marvellous, funny, irresistible, and encourage you back into life and more mistakes?

Of course I'm selfless.

This book is about sex because I have talked to a lot of mature women, some happy, some temporarily (one hopes) not. Some successful, others comfortably ordinary, but all of them out there trying, not giving up.

And all of them discovering, as I did, that sex, that wonderful, driving, life-enhancing force need not come to an abrupt halt on one's fortieth birthday whether or not one is half of a couple.

Any woman now in her forties grew up Cinderella-conditioned; Mr Right came along, followed by a mortgage and babies, and when you were twenty you were totally certain that by the time the mortgage got paid off only senility would await. Of course forty-five was going to be old, as old as parents – and look how dull their lives were.

For better or worse (and oh, the refined cynicism of that majestic, biblical phrase) society has changed, and a hell of a lot of those virginal twenty-year-old ladies now find themselves on their own, children grown and husband gone. The days when a man's motto was 'keep their bellies up and their heels (and that means of their shoes) down' are past.

Easy divorce and the contraceptive pill seem to have made a better marriage than the human guinea-pigs but at least the average woman of forty is no longer a tooth-less old hag mourning over half a dozen tiny gravestones. She is more likely to be a confident, healthy, working human being who has seriously taken to her heart every-thing the cosmetics and fashion industry wish to sell her. As an old, instinctive left-winger I submit willingly to the charms of the capitalists who have persuaded me I don't have to grow old gracefully.

For any woman who has raised a family, a job that has automatically involved a certain amount of self-sacrifice, having the time and money to spend on herself is an exhilarating and renewing experience – or should be. It is up to her whether she interprets her new status as freedom or loneliness, whether she indulges in positive or negative thinking. You can guess which one I recommend.

So here we are.

Divorced. Forced to be financially independent, luckily free of the fear of pregnancy. Randy. And forty-odd.

What to do?

Well, we could look for someone else on the rebound from a broken marriage and take on him, his teenage children and all of their problems.

We could settle for the once or twice a week mistress

role to somebody's dissatisfied husband and suffer lonely weekends and holiday times.

We could try to steal another woman's husband and cause pain to a whole family.

We could become a fag-hag, the idolized centre of attention at flash parties who goes home alone, or with the occasional bisexual.

We could become spinsters and keep a cat instead of our pussies warm.

We could even contemplate whether or not we have lesbian tendencies. Or . . . we could break almost the last social/sexual taboo and take a younger lover, better still a series of younger lovers, and thoroughly enjoy sex at that age when a woman is at her intellectual and sexual peak.

To choose this pioneering path does take a bit of courage, more than a bit in fact. First there is one's own sense of guilt, even shame, to be overcome. Then there are the attitudes of other people.

Society has for centuries regarded the mature predatory male, the seducer of young flesh, as a hero. He may be a bit of a scallywag but he is the living proof of man's ability to maintain virility. Envious his friends may be, but indulgent they are to the point of admiration. But when the roles are reversed and the woman is the senior partner, society has been far from titillated; the woman is by tradition thought to be making a fool of herself (they forget that older men do too) and the young man is frequently viewed with suspicion . . . is he a gigolo or is he seeking a mother figure?

She is often made to feel cheap : seldom do you find admiration for the woman who has 'pulled' a younger man, the acknowledgment that *she* has kept *her* sexuality. And yet the last five years have seen the gossip columns swell with stories of glamorous older women, usually in their forties or early fifties, finding happiness and fulfilment with younger men.

Diana Dors, Sheila Hancock, Nyree Dawn Porter – all are married to men ten years their junior. Louise Fletcher has happily found Morgan Mason, son of James, who is twenty years her junior; Rachel Roberts is fifteen years senior to the beautiful Darren Ramirez. Even the last couple to be married at Caxton Hall were separated by twelve years, she was thirty-six and he twenty-four.

There are many other celebrated figures from the past. When Marie Lloyd married Ben Dillon she was forty and he was twenty-two. Colette lived contentedly with her Willi, twenty years younger, and wrote the most exquisite tragedies of love between a younger man and an older woman, *Cheri* and *The Last of Cheri*. Edith Piaf had young lovers till the day she died.

When it came to recording contemporary examples, I have to admit I was disappointed in the number of well-known couples who were reluctant to talk about themselves. It seemed to me a marvellous opportunity to stand up for something they obviously believed in; did their refusal mean that the taboo is still there in their minds? Didn't they realize that their actions could have as profound an influence on the breaking of conventional attitudes as that of the pop stars of the Sixties who openly rebelled against marriage and made living together cheerfully acceptable for the young of today, be they students or factory workers? Then I thought again, and reflected on the way Princess Margaret was crucified in the Press for her relationship with Roddy Llewellyn. Whether their relationship was amorous or just that of two people who enjoyed each other's company is of no importance. The world wallowed in a scandal. An older woman and a younger man! Shocking! Scorn was poured on both of them. She was derided for preferring the company of a different generation to her peers, literally, and he was decried as an ambitious dilettante, using a woman to clamber to fame. Of course intolerance lives.

For the less exalted of us the problems may not be so great, but they are still there. I should know, I have been researching them diligently, conscientiously, for several years, and my own findings have been authenticated by the many women I have talked to. Admittedly the role of the older woman with the young lover is easier for rich or successful women, but the number of independent women for whom it could make sense is on the increase. A few of those I interviewed, as you will discover, *are* famous. The others are exuberant, exceptional women in the sense that they are prepared to live their *own* lives – but are otherwise ordinary people.

It was during a particularly delicious piece of research that the idea for this book came to me; as ever in my favourite haunt of wisdom and wish fulfilment – bed.

Reluctant to extricate myself from the warmth of the body beside me I allowed myself to be led into one of those gentle, funny, morning-after exchanges of confidence that re-weave the patterns of the past.

Now age – mine that is – has not been among my favourite subjects for several years and it gave me no pleasure as the conversation drifted on to realize that on the day I had first strapped the elastic of my grammar school hat under my chin my lover was as yet unborn! But then it got worse. Listening to him I discovered that as I was giving birth to my third child my new lover was just entering secondary school, and when I was getting divorced he was embarking on his first youthful mistake; marrying too young.

You note, I hope, I said 'listening'. I kept my calculations to myself. He was by no means my first young lover but until that moment I had trained myself to be deliberately unaware of a man's age, indeed, had rather coarsely assumed that if they were big enough they were old enough, an attitude well suited to the light-hearted traveller through life who believes that a cheerful, lusty, one night stand does more good than harm. In those situations reality finds no haven; good looks, charm, laughter, opportunity are the only qualifications necessary. Desire ignores any difference in age.

But what if the fun of the instant celebration of lust should turn gradually, tenderly and sweetly into a real relationship ... can the age difference still be ignored? After all a relationship is more than the give and take of sexual pleasure, more than the temporary thrill of acquiring a new drinking and dancing partner. Desert island situations apart a relationship involves more than two people, it affects friends, family and, in this case, the prejudices of society.

The women I have talked to discussed many aspects of these problems, and being of differing characters their reactions and solutions varied. Many of them did not want their real names used, sometimes to protect a former relationship, sometimes to protect a present one, and sometimes to protect the guilty ... themselves. This request I have honoured.

Some of the interviews were hilarious and some were sad, but all were given with great honesty and I should like here to state my gratitude to all the women who opened up their lives to me – and, of course, to all the young men whose contributions have been gratefully received!

I should also like to point out that this book is not aimed at the lucky numbers of happily married women ... though it may do no harm to give the old man a twinge of anxiety by leaving the title around! I hope this book will be of some help to the multitudes of women who are standing alone mid-way into life. In the words of that life-celebrating song from *Cabaret*:

> What good is sitting alone in your room,
> Come hear the music play,
> Life is a cabaret, old chum,
> Come to the cabaret.

I

THE TURNING POINT

How many women, approaching or in their forties, long to re-shape their destiny? To escape the routine of their lives, whether it be the domestic round, the daily commuting train or bus, or the dreariness of a meaningless social existence? Even happily married women, content to be the manipulating factor in their husband's and children's lives sometimes long to stand out from the crowd on their own; to be recognized as something other than John's wife and the children's mother. To be people in their own right. And how many have the courage to do it, to accept the challenge when opportunity comes rapping on the door?

There are so many excuses at hand: 'the children, an undomesticated husband, pets, the garden, no money to spare for training!' – all these can be marshalled for the defence. Sometimes these excuses are valid, the timing of the offer of a job, an adventurous holiday, the chance to learn a new skill, can be inopportune . . . but all too often it is fear that holds a woman back. Fear of change, the rut is too comfortable. There is the possibility of failure and looking foolish out there in the big wide world.

The influences on the shape of the second half of a woman's life are many; environment, status, skills, family and financial circumstances all play their part. But the greatest influence is her own; in her ability or inability to steer herself through the mid-life passage will be the difference between a vigorous and fruitful future or a wasting of twenty precious years.

The turning point of a woman's life has usually taken a lot longer to arrive than is obvious on the surface. The strong, sparkling women in their forties seem to be the ones who have used their thirties as a period of re-assessment, they have explored their own limitations and made an attempt to remedy some of the deficiencies. Some have turned to self-help books, tried transcendental meditation, yoga or resurrecting their pre-marital talents like painting or music. Others have taken evening classes to learn a new skill, dance classes to keep trim or learned to drive a car. There may be no immediate benefit obvious in these activities but they are preparations for a future when a woman's whole life no longer pivots round the family. When school hours no longer dictate the shape of a woman's life she is mentally ready to seize on any opportunity, maybe to take her first job or upgrade a career that needs more attention. Even if the planning is only semi-conscious with no direct ambition in mind the energy being poured into a new direction will not be wasted in the restlessness and depression that hits so many housewives when the years ahead loom up like a void.

Some women have learned a lot about themselves through their children, keeping up with their interests, and many have gone through the hell of a broken marriage and have had to go out into the world on their own whether they wanted to or not. The days when giving birth to two or three children was a meal ticket for life are over. Society has changed and with it the women.

But not all. Sadly, some women still cling to the idea that their reproductive years are the only ones of importance. They have done their duty to life and should be repaid in bricks, mortar and maintenance. There was correspondence in *The Guardian* last year about the rights of wives and mothers when the man in their lives wanted to move on. The arguments were pitiless and pitiful; shrouded in blame, financial fears, the problem of the children's schooling, indignation, and not overlooking the agony of rejection. Nobody once considered the opportunity for change. The inference was, quite frankly, that the woman would be better off if the man, the husband and father, were dead rather than have a second chance at happiness with another woman.

Not for one moment would I underrate the misery and upheaval of divorce but neither can I bring myself to pour out paeans of praise for a household kept together by righteous hatred. Everybody misses out; the husband with his renewed vigour for love and life, the children, to whom schooling is only a part of life, and the woman – oh, the great loser with an empty man and an empty life ahead of her yet, the acceptance of circumstances, the fact that people can and do change, could give her true independence, coupled with unforeseeable chances to develop as a human being.

Of course it isn't easy for a woman to let go of a man she loves and has formed a pattern of life with. It is a shock, but one from which she will recover; she may moan, whimper and grieve but recover she will, and empty though life will seem at first, eventually it will be filled. For some the solution may be voluntary work, and for that society should be grateful, for others it may be a job that brings companionship, independence and a new outlook, one aspect of which must to consider what to do for her new sex life.

Given the right mental attitude, a woman at forty is luckier than her male equivalent; he has already exploited his early energies, she, if she has prepared herself during her late thirties, has her energies banked and raring to go.

Lack of self-confidence is the enemy, fear is the great destroyer and forty seems to be its crucible; it is the moment to decide whether the cup is half-empty or half-full. So you'll never be a prima ballerina, have thirty-four-inch hips again or get to screw Warren Beatty, but there are still plenty of other things to do, and twenty to thirty years in which to do them. So, you've got a few wrinkles, character lines . . . try looking out a few old snapshots and see how vacant that youthful face looked. And the boobs don't point in the northerly direction they once did? The stretch-marks look like an Ordnance Survey map, so what? There is still no need to be overweight, your body has simply fulfilled its early function and must now be kept fit to fulfil its later one. You are a woman not a girl, you have *earned* your life-signs, they are part of the human being that wants to go on living and experiencing. Few, very few, people are perfectly formed.

Facing up to forty is a second chance at a bite of the apple and if it is Eve's apple all the better. Everything else, career, looks and opportunities for adventure will fall into place.

The time has come for women to shake off the shackles of convention, to throw off cloying romanticism and to be practical and realistic about their sex lives. According to the women I have talked to, the sex drive of a woman in her forties, and her ability to enjoy and give sexual satisfaction, are greater than when she was twenty; she is freer, uninhibited, no longer afraid of her own sexuality, and she should be experienced enough to handle desire without love, when needs must. Some people may consider that last sentence harsh, tough. Life usually has been just that to women who are currently single in their forties. Divorced or widowed, they have had to learn self-reliance, the youthful dreams of eternal love have been shattered, they have made mistakes and watched others make mistakes. They have often had to assume the male role both inside and outside the family, why not in sex too? If they have reached the stage in their lives where they can regard sex as a pleasure, a sensual pleasure like a good meal, why complicate it with commitment?

Learning to enjoy sex for its own sake is an important step in a woman's life – mentally as much as physically. The woman's attitude to herself changes radically as she learns to disregard the opinions of family, friends, neighbours and others. Her new-found self-approval is the consummation of the knowledge that the body that has been out on loan for twenty-odd years, in the roles of mother, wife, daughter-in-law, has now returned to its original owner. It is hers alone now, hers to look after, hers to use for pleasure and enjoyment. She, the owner, is responsible for its upkeep, maintenance and appearance, and from now on she is entitled to bestow its love, lust, or presence whenever and to whoever she pleases. After all is said and done the body is the only thing we truly own; houses will belong to others, jewellery and money will be owned by others, furniture, gardens, sunsets will all be there when we are gone, but our enjoyment of our own bodies, our brains and memories, cannot be taken from us. To waste this complicated, mysterious piece of mechanism that we move around in is, to me, a great sin.

Self-love is not a sin. It is self-hate that produces envy, vindictiveness, small-mindedness; self-love is self-acceptance, the knowledge of imperfections, of room for improvement and the time in which to achieve it. Being relaxed about her faults without exaggerating her virtues can make a woman very desirable company at all levels.

Being desired as a woman is still very restorative to the woman who has been wounded by life. Even if she secretly hopes that there will one day be another real relationship with someone to love, it would be foolish to deny herself the delights of temporary, even frivolous associations. Light-hearted, unpossessive affairs can teach a woman, particularly the formerly monogamous woman, a great deal about the control of her emotions. Falling lightly in love just for the fun of it can be a very refreshing experience, since the happiness of short-lived affairs is totally dependent on the absence of expectations and responsibilities. Neither party is under any illusions, heads are kept, hearts are only fluttering and bodies are satisfied. When the bubble bursts there should be no recriminations (though self-congratulations for good conduct are forgivable) and lots of warm memories. The apprentice grown woman is learning to live for the moment and her progress will probably take her through many such affairs; her hold on her lovers may be ephemeral but her hold on herself will be strengthened. And should she one day become more deeply involved, in a mutually loving relationship, she will have more to offer than a bruised ego and gratitude.

But where to start? By accepting all invitations, whether they look dull or devious. An invitation to tea or drinks with an elderly couple can lead to a discovery of books, music, or the kind of history hidden in personal lives. Anything that opens the mind is an addition to life and practising your single-state charm will teach you that you still have much to offer regardless of your ex-husband's opinions. Don't waste new friendships with bemoaning the past, realise that there is much to learn and take a big step forward. Also, really old people are born interferers and are bound to want to introduce you to someone new. You are on the move.

The devious invitations will come, almost without doubt, from your ex-husband's best friends who have secretly fancied you for years, or your best friends' husbands, who have ditto. Use them. Use them ruthlessly to get you into places, to meet people and become known as a free agent. Never lose the opportunity to state your escort's status, crushing his hopes further with a compliment to his kindness, and never, ever get trapped into a conversation about your ex. Malice after a couple of drinks is unbecoming in a woman and tears are a drag.

When the invitations run out, and the devious ones will when the wives get wind of them, it is time to start going it alone. Do anything; take a train or a bus to a place you have never seen, a stately home, a town you have read about. Go to a gallery, a concert or a lecture on your own, it doesn't matter, the point is that you have chosen to do something and achieved it by yourself. You may feel nervous and self-conscious but luckily nobody can see the palpitations of the heart. You are taking a training course in self-confidence and even paratroopers have been known to do nasty things in their trousers when faced with their first jump.

One of the simplest ways to change from the inside is to apply this mental trick; each time you hear yourself say

'I've always ... worn my hair like this; bought my clothes at that shop; read this newspaper; gone to such-and-such a place for my holiday' ... make a decision to be different in the future. A new hairdresser will look at your potential with a stranger's eyes, so will a new shop. An unfamiliar newspaper can present fresh opinions to you, and the world is full of amazing places to explore and discover, and people to meet. It is all preparation for the new you and your new life.

Taking your first young lover is curiously like losing your virginity, especially if you have been part of a monogamous marriage. It is also oddly like plucking up the courage to go into a pub on your own for the first time, or your first day in a new job. You feel shy, self-conscious and vulnerable. Afterwards you can feel anything from guilty, used or liberated. It is up to you to adapt, and adjust in your own time.

Take it easy on yourself. You are not the first woman to slip into bed with a man who was still at school when you were already a bride. Marie Lloyd, Edith Piaf and Colette did it, and I shouldn't think Madame Recamier was too much of a slouch on the couch either. As you will read in this book, lots of women decide in their forties that they prefer young men as lovers and companions.

I did, and I am glad that I did. I have had a lot of fun, a sprinkling of saucy adventures, learned that at times life can be arid and lonely, also that there are many forms of love that do not involve possessiveness. No one being can own another, but the sharing of a day or night can be a loving link across continents or years. I have loved, temporarily, many men, and lusted after more. Both feelings have been reciprocated, temporarily. Through them, the fact of their being in my life at the time, I have been able to return to love ... not temporarily, I hope, but who knows? The time has not been wasted.

Looking back on my own turning point I realize it was a long time in the forming. Like many people of my generation I married young, had children straight away, got divorced too young and sought out a career, my devotion to which helped ruin my next common-law marriage. At the start of my forties I was successful and alone, my children happily independent and either leaving or preparing to leave home.

For approximately eighteen months I had been looking at young men at parties, pubs and clubs with a speculative eye. They all seemed so charming, friendly and flirtatious, their clothes so sexy and bold, their eyes bright with instant promise. At the end of each social encounter I would drag myself shamefaced away. How could I, I scolded myself, even think about them at my great age? How dare I lust after these handsome young men who must be only interested in girls the same age as my daughters? It was disgusting, wrong. My mirror agreed with me.

I sought companionship amongst my peers and finally found one, a colleague, a succesful journalist who could talk shop with the best, make love splendidly, make me laugh and generally add zest to my life. I had been saved from the distasteful error of making a fool of myself over a young man.

The affair had been flourishing several weeks. We were with friends in a bar when the subject turned to age. It is the one subject that can shut me up but I was listening with half an ear when I heard my beloved announce 'I'm thirty-one.' For a moment I thought he was joking. I tried to sound casual but sheer disbelief was in my voice. 'What did you say?' His face was filled with wicked delight at my incredulous expression. 'I'm thirty-one' he repeated.

It took me days and a great deal of sweet talk to recover. When I did I was delighted. I had broken the age barrier, had been truly shown how unimportant the age gap was. I had been foolishly worrying about the years behind me, indulging in the vague, primeval belief that woman's function on this planet was to have children and that after that she was finished. Evolutionary, my dear Watson. I must have been daft. Revolutionary I became, as I began to plot the pleasures of the years ahead. I joined the second half of the twentieth century fast. I was no Victorian crone wrecked by twenty years of child-bearing, miscarriages and death, I was heiress to my own future, to do with as I pleased.

The beloved turned out to be a villain, but a lovely one. He had known about our age difference and had not cared. He had set me free from my own deep-rooted prejudices and we have been friends ever since.

Just how deep those prejudices had been came back to me as I talked to Erica on the subject. After eighteen years of marriage her husband had announced that he was leaving her and their three children to live with a young girl of twenty-two. All of their friends were shocked. But all of them, including myself, were even more shocked when Erica found herself a young man of twenty-four. We saw her flashing around in her racing-green convertible, laughing, happy and cared for after years of that corroding semi-neglect that augurs the end of family life. We stood around wondering what on earth she could see in him, he was so *young*. We couldn't talk to him, *we* had nothing in common. 'Actually,' says Erica, 'I didn't fancy young men when I was in my early thirties but suddenly they started to look so pretty. I was devastated by the way Sean dressed, it was probably very ordinary but I thought he was a knockout. I know everyone was giggling their heads off but I didn't care. I was flattered by his attention, a little embarrassed, too. He was so very excited by all the things I took for granted, going to restaurants like Wheelers where I had been a customer for years, or to the Colony Room Club. The other side of the coin was going out with *his* friends to ghastly things like the Pink Floyd. Then I felt 190.

'But he was marvellous with my children. For them it was like having an older brother, and they played crazy games and liked the same sort of music. It lasted six months, one long, lovely, hot summer, and it restored me. Then it just petered out.

'After that there were a lot of young men. It wasn't that I chose them deliberately, just that all the people I mixed with of my own generation were people I had known forever. Even now I hardly meet anybody new of my own age. And I wasn't about to start going to bed with them, none of us would dream of it. It was a fact that the only new people I met, and still do, were much younger . . . the next generation wave was coming into town. Doesn't that sound awful! But they still look much prettier to me, the young men, and their bodies are better.

'I looked at my ex the other day and remembered that every time I saw him after he left me my heart would die, I lusted after him so much. I'm fond of him now but I couldn't fancy him in a million years.'

Erica has been happily living with a man ten years her junior for the last eight years.

27

Gloria, an American, was another deserted wife and mother, heartbroken and tortured with a sense of failure made doubly ironic as her husband of ten years had left his previous wife and children to marry her.

'One day I realized I was being an absolute twit. It was time to give up my fairy-tale attitude to life, love and marriage. It came to me while I was talking to a woman friend who is a sociologist. I had been having a lot of frivolous relationships, mostly based on drink, pretty unsatisfactory. From a conventional point of view I suppose I had been wildly promiscuous. Anyhow the conversation turned round to how long you could expect anything to last and she said casually "two years is fair . . ." and I had still been thinking in terms of forever and ever!

'So I decided to stop looking for another husband and security, and to stop thinking about my age and do a little cradle-robbing. I felt very, very naughty but I planned to seduce Bill whom I had met through work. An evening at the theatre with dinner at a little place round the corner where even he could afford to pay his share of the bill! But I was thwarted. He had shopped for a spaghetti carbonara and a bottle of red plonk. We have been together ever since, three and a half years. How old is he? Seventeen years my junior.'

Not all women wait till their forties, some start practising while still in their thirties, a situation I deplore. After all, if the older women are going to get younger – as I think will happen in the Eighties – those dolly-birds of the Sixties will be looking over *their* shoulders soon. We late developers had better get a move on.

Take Eva, for example; a most sophisticated copy-writer

from Canada. 'The first time I ever had a sexual involvement with a younger man was when I was thirty-two. I had recommended a builder whom I had never met (but had heard could deliver the goods) to a friend of mine in the flat below. He came to see me because she wasn't in, and my God, did he produce the goods! You see, when this very beautiful young man appeared at the door I was wearing my bathrobe, and as my neighbour wasn't in, the sensible and courteous thing was for him to wait in my flat – and within half an hour, I'm afraid we were off. He was twenty-one, though his age never really occurred to me. Afterwards I did think it was amusing.

'Age does occur to me now. I have a close friend with an extremely beautiful young son and I desperately want him on a casually decadent basis. He is only eighteen and I wonder whether I ought to. Funnily enough although I have been at it now for ten years this is the first time I have had any conscience about it – probably because all the others were accidents and this one is deliberate.

'Mostly I think the older woman/younger man relationships must be OK because everyone's getting more out of it than they otherwise would have done. It is one of the few involvements available where nobody's being screwed, except in the sense you both are. Nobody's the loser. The boy is gaining experience, the woman is gaining pleasure. I think the older woman can teach them how to relax and enjoy it . . . they are all suffering from an excess of vigour at that age. I honestly think that every young man I have been to bed with has probably *enjoyed* sex a bloody sight more when I have finished with him.'

It is Molly Parkin, the author of wickedly erotic novels, who has the most outrageous excuse for the turning point in a woman's life. Long before she met her husband Patrick who is seven years her junior, she had nobly sacrificed herself and her honour to save a young man from a fate worse than death. A friend of hers. A fella.

'I wasn't at all interested in young men, but I went to a party with a poofy friend of mine and there was this good-looking boy. "That's going to be mine tonight," he said, and I told him "No, you can't, he hasn't had anything yet," but he repeated "That's going to be mine," so I said "I'm not going to let you do it" and I pulled the boy. He was only sixteen, poor little sod. I was thirty-four. After that I went back to my team of three regulars who were around my age or a bit older until I met Patrick on holiday. He was meant to be my holiday romance. I did invite him to join the team, but he saw the rest of them off.'

Niké Williams, the exotic fashion editor of *Honey* magazine, was quick to the trough too.

'Women waste far too many years making up their minds to lead their own lives their own way. They are still brainwashed by male chauvinist attitudes and guilt . . . if you fuck, you are a tart. I have to own up that I got into my first fling with a young man as the result of a dare. There were three of us, two older women and myself sitting in a pub near a health farm, where I had gone to lose the weight I had put on after the break-up of a love affair with a man in my own age group. Anyhow we were sitting there and the women's eyes were out on stalks gazing at this staggering young lad behind the bar, they were really fancying him, and a few gins after four days on lemon juice and their energy was rampant! They didn't have the courage to make a pass at him themselves but they egged me on, well, I've never been one to pass up a chance so I chatted him up till closing time. We went swimming naked at midnight. . . . The next day he came round to my room at the health farm with a bunch of roses and a bottle of champagne. Who could resist style *and* good looks? I didn't. And the rest is history – we had a whole glorious year and a half together. He was nineteen when I met him and I was thirty-four, fifteen years between us. The next one was even younger, only eighteen and even more handsome. I find myself terribly attracted by their innocence. It's something I want to treasure, never deflate.'

There can be no doubt about it, the woman who can be honest with herself has found the key to her own freedom. If some of these stories, and others in the ensuing chapters, sound flippant, they are not. They have been lived, digested and absorbed by women who have the guts to laugh at their own mishaps and carry on with life.

Glenn Wilson, of the Institute of Psychiatry, and consultant for a computerised match-making service, states quite baldly that there is, in our society, a surplus of older single women and young single men, and that 'the salvation of the older woman is probably going to be in the male's exploratory drive, his need for variety and novelty. A lot of younger men are curious about what an older woman can do for them.'

We, the women of the Western world, are living in a new age, and we have the scientists to thank for it. Firstly, they have invented weapons of war so terrible that a whole generation of young men are no longer forced to become cannon fodder. Secondly, they have invented contraception which allows women to reach the ripe young age of forty with teeth, hair and bodies more or less intact . . . the times when women gave birth to a child a year, ruinous to their health, are part of history for most of our present society. The demise of the nuclear family is the birth of the New Woman of the Eighties. Being a romantic in the philosophical sense, I am quite convinced that Mother Nature always intended to reward us for our pains, and the freedom to enjoy sex for its own sake is her gift.

If sex looms large in our lives, and pray heaven it will continue to do so, it is because, like Everest (give or take an inch or two) it is there. Some people can live without it and good luck to them, that doesn't mean to say the rest of us have to.

Celibacy is never thrust upon us.

Ponder that, and I hope you see the joke, and consider the sad, bad tale of Anne Cumming, the author of *The Love Habit*, the wicked story of a sexually dynamic grandmother whose bed ventures ranged over three continents. Anne, on her fiftieth birthday, had been discarded by two husbands and a long-term lover who reverted to homosexuality, and announced that she was giving up sex forever. Thoughtfully her friends provided her with the present that was to change her life, a beautiful young man. She struggled gamely with her resolution and came sensibly to the conclusion that the fact that she had given up the search for Mr Right need not prevent her from enjoying a whole series of Mr Nows. Ten fun-packed years and a best-seller later she can say, 'One of the things I like about young men is that they are unattached and when it is over no one is hurt, in fact I took to this life-style at fifty because I had been hurt so much. I am still good friends with all my boys and I really don't want other women's husbands, I know the pain caused by unfaithfulness and never want to be its cause.'

That was interesting because the week previously I had been standing in a Mayfair club with Pat, a big, blonde ex-singer of fifty-five who lives in Malta with a young man of twenty-four. They have been living together since he was sixteen. Sitting beside her was a life-long woman friend who had never been able to reconcile herself to Pat's love affair.

'I couldn't do it,' she murmured, 'how can you take off your clothes in front of someone so young?'

'I keep telling *her* to turn off the light,' said the un-repentant Pat, 'but I like to see the person I am in bed with,' replied the friend.

I asked her if she were married. No, she wasn't. Then the lover she enjoyed with the light on was somebody else's husband. Yes. She genuinely couldn't understand that I found Pat's moral standards infinitely preferable to her own. Pat, with her generous sexuality, was to her, dis-gusting, immoral.

But there, everybody has their own moral standards, which brings us to another dilemma of the turning point ... no woman likes to think of herself as promiscuous and it is certainly not a label she wishes to acquire; how is she to maintain a delicate balance between the new-found joyous freedom of choice and the nagging doubt of being used?

Phyllis, an actress turned painter whose list of conquests in her early days would make the average woman drool with envy says firmly, 'As you get older it is easier to be honest with yourself and with the men. I know when I am using a man and when he is using me. When I was younger I think I used to put on an act in bed, but I find sex so much better now and I can see it more realistically. It's fairly momentary so it's not worth having bad feelings afterwards. If you feel used, you are used; and it's time to move on. I don't see any other alternative but to go on the way I am, picking the occasional new body or face. It's very important not to allow yourself to be treated badly . . . and a lot easier to tell them the truth when you are older.'

I agree with her. Quite frankly I would rather be called promiscuous than frigid any day, and I'm not all that keen on celibacy either, though a little lull between bouts is a useful period for inner growth, to catch up with old friendships and generally sort out one's progress. There is no logical reason why the modern woman should not have a variety of partners, it is certainly healthier for her emotional development; a succession of young lovers should be regarded as a tribute to her sensuality and to her ability to handle her own life with delicacy and aplomb. Only ludicrous prejudice applies the word promiscuous to such women – it is never used about men.

There are risks of course. Getting hurt is one of them, usually only a slight case of wounded pride. Catching a dose is another, but that is something that could come from any age-group – including an unfaithful husband. We can all make mistakes; the enchanting young lover can turn out to be neurotic, possessive, a heavy drinker or even married. Few women will make my classic error of judgment and pick up a young man who turned out to be a mass-murderer, but that's another story.

Laughing at your own mistakes, knowing that you will live to gloat over your triumphs another day is all part of being a grown woman. Nobody's perfect. But a warm, vigorous love of life seemed to be the common denominator amongst the older women I interviewed, particularly those in their sixties who have been 'at it' since their early forties. Once past their own turning point, which was basically discarding other people's ideas on the running of their lives, they have tackled their lives and loves with audacity, humour and style. And they are still too busy enjoying themselves for rancour or regrets.

2

THE ADVANTAGES

There is one glaringly, gorgeously obvious, indisputable fact about having an affair with a younger man. Sex. You get plenty of it. Morning, noon and night, and anywhere you please. Not for them the formality of the bedroom only. The joy of an ardent young lover is that he wants it *now* and it doesn't matter if you are in the bathroom, the kitchen, a field, a shop doorway, or in a car, on a plane, train or building site.

And it's the best tonic in the world, both physically and mentally. A woman going out to meet her young lover is not likely to arrive complaining of a headache; she will be fit, trim, with shiny hair and sparkling eyes, ready for anything from a football match to a discotheque. Piped full of vitamins she may be but slurping with chocolate cake she ain't. With a career and life-style to give her confidence she knows she can be a lively and entertaining companion both in bed and out. Maybe life has reduced her circumstances from lady of the manor to the owner of little more than a bed-sit. Maybe she genuinely misses having a husband and children to fuss over. But life has to go on, and there is no point in bemoaning the past.

It is the present that counts. And that includes enjoying the moment with any young man who crosses the horizon. Gone forever are the days of being disturbed mid-action by a whimpering baby or wondering if the pubescent child in the next room can hear the bed creaking. Gone too are all the familiar routines of mammoth shopping loads, endless meals to be cooked and cleaned-up after, worrying about school clothes, unexplainable temperatures, late homecomings, of going to P.T.A. meetings and sitting through school concerts.

Of course it is hard at first. It takes courage to go out and get a job, to become a minion, for a woman who has spent fifteen to twenty years ruling her own domain. Especially at the time when tradition has schooled a woman to consider her usefulness as a person over and done with.

'Who will want me at my age?' is far too frequently the first cry, but a daft one considering the woman in question has, in fact, just reached the age of many desirable qualities: realism, compassion, even wisdom; and certainly her sexual peak. In an ideal marriage this would be the time for the original couple to rediscover each other, to enjoy once again the company of the person they wed twenty years ago. But the chances are, in our current society, that the woman in her mid-forties has been a lone parent for some years and she faces the prospect of the end of her caring years, her children leaving home, with fear and dread.

This is the moment for realism to conquer the temptation to look back with sentiment. The past was never all wonderful and neither will the future be, there will be pleasures and pains as there always have been. But the very least we can do for ourselves is accept some of the pleasures offered, and one of them is the continued enjoyment and use of our own bodies.

37

So, you have spent twenty-odd years of your adulthood looking after a family? Now you can spend the next twenty-odd looking after yourself. That money that always went on school uniforms can go on your own back . . . and so can you. Fate, whether through bad luck, mismanagement or your own needs, has given you Time and Freedom, wonderful gifts.

Sure, we all fear old age because it presages death . . . but there are many, many young persons lying six feet under who would be only too delighted to be facing the problems of adapting to being forty-odd. The world may well expect you to settle down and wait for the grandchildren to arrive, but what a terrible waste . . . and waste, in my opinion, is one of the great deadly sins.

I seem to have forgotten the others.

I like being a woman more than I liked being a girl and so, I find, do the other women I meet who are still enjoying a vigorous and sometimes varied sex life. They have fun and they exude their renewed zest for life for the world to share; a room lights up when they enter. Their conversation is amusing, outrageous, interesting, their lines are truly laughter lines and their bodies move with a sensuality that demonstrates the relaxing of earlier inhibitions and the discovery of unfettered sex. Compare them with the conventional matron whose husband has long since lost interest in her, who has grown stout on gin and sadness, and one can soon see who is getting most out of life. The sexually mature woman, one who does not confuse love with lust, men-friends with marriage and mortgages, is a self-assured woman who has learned to compartmentalise her life; her career and her bed habits are no threat to each other. These women do not look to men for protection. If they get knocked back by circumstance they come out of the corner fighting for themselves and yet they are wonderfully feminine, thus allowing the men in their lives, the casual and the important ones, to be fully integrated males. Their style and personality are radiantly louche.

And the adventures they have!

The outrageous Molly Parkin celebrated an impromptu and wildly satisfying romp in a field with her then lover Patrick by having her hair dyed green to match the grass. No wonder he married her! And, as she remarks with her unabashed candour, 'He is the only man I have ever had a poke with through my period. I think that's awfully good. Men of my generation never do. When I used to ring my lovers with the pains they would always arrange to meet in a restaurant instead of coming round for a poke. Patrick always says 'So what?' and pops it in just the same. I was flabbergasted by that but actually you are very horny when you have your period, so afterwards he just goes and washes it off. Lovely.'

Molly is absolutely right, a man who is not upset by normal bodily functions will be at ease with the warts in your personality too.

But stupid attitudes remain. Recently I went into a chemist's and queued, uncaring, in front of a counter display of condoms; glossily packed and in many varieties. I asked the assistant for a packet of tampons. He waved me to the far end of the shop. 'We keep them there so as not to embarrass our lady customers,' he confided. Whilst I was falling about laughing my lover solemnly walked the length of the shop and bought them for me. The incident was just another absurd demonstration of the conformist attitude of women being shy little violets, ashamed of what goes on 'down there.' Real women are not like that.

Martha Hill, the fashion designer and creator of the most effective herbal skin care cosmetics I have ever come across, is now well into her sixties and reminiscing. 'I met an old lover the other day and we were remembering the time when we ruined the back seat of his Rolls with spur marks, he was in full hunting gear but we just couldn't wait. He was ten years younger than me, we were always pulling the car off the road. He said that everything about me was luscious, what a lovely word.'

What a marvellous memory to have. Had Martha said 'no,' an unlikely event according to her conversation, two people would have been deprived of a moment to cherish all their lives.

It is this urgency and spontaneity that lends enchantment to an act that to the more conservative (or less opportunist) seems sordid. How else would the Mile High Club, where the couple have it off in the lavatory of an aeroplane, having gained such a glamorous reputation? Standing giggling in a darkened shop doorway or having a quick one over the office desk adds an element of naughtiness that allows both parties to behave like kids again, making sex the fun it should be. Sure it's a far cry from 'the whole earth moved' syndrome and the seriousness of the Big O but it is lovely and wicked and pagan, especially as it has nothing to do with having nowhere to go; it isn't a necessity as in infidelity, it's an extra when there is the certainty of a large double bed at home.

It's as much a part of love as paying the mortgage and an instant erection is a greater compliment than a bunch of flowers (though the two together can be very beguiling). Such moments are also worth relating. You seldom find good, honest, rampantly sexual women discussing the price of greens. If, at a social gathering of any kind, you see two or three women, talking, laughing and giving out no help signals to the men in the room, you can bet your sweet life they are talking about cock. I reckon they talk more about it than men do, women love to relate their adventures and swop information. Many a pretty man has failed the hot-chat test and many a quiet one has gone off with the prize once his prowess has been thoroughly discussed. At these entertaining conclaves you hear Jane telling of the night her lover screwed her in every room in the house carrying her from bedroom to bathroom to kitchen on the end of his prick. And Sally will contribute her tale of how she had to scramble out of the bathroom window because the young man who told her he couldn't get any woman to go to bed with him because his member was so enormous was actually speaking the truth! Out they all tumble, the hilarious stories of one night stands; the magic night on the cliff tops of Sydney, having it off in a Lotus parked in the shadows of the columns of Hyde Park Corner late on Christmas Eve, of getting caught out in a crypt in Mexico and trying to scramble over a six foot railing to escape only to be trapped by one's own yellow clogs and a middle-aged lack of agility. Any secret doubts about the impropriety of one's past behaviour disappears in gales of laughter as Jinny recalls the night she said 'yes' to a pop star in Las Vegas and found herself installed in a suite with two large, armed bodyguards on the other side of the door.

And Eva relates: 'I was on holiday in this English colony and had been told about Harry who apparently was so devastating that all the girls wanted to slash their wrists when he discarded them. So I thought, right, I'll fuck anybody but Harry. Predictably I met Harry on the first night and he was absolutely fabulous. My kneecaps buckled, but I had promised to be a good girl so off I went to a restaurant and a couple of discos and there I met this young fella whose name I didn't inquire after – we ended up on the beach where he screwed me silly until eight in the morning : we had been driving at seventy miles an hour with full glasses of brandy in our hands, the usual first-night-of-a-holiday drunken stuff. The following morning I was woken by my hostess with the news that I had been summoned to the Harringtons for drinks. I was delivered there at a quarter to one and fifteen minutes later Mrs Harrington was saying, "Now where is that lazy little beast, he has been drinking all night but he must get up." Five minutes later he appeared in his pyjamas – my companion of the night before, the devastating Harry's son . . . all of nineteen summers.'

Holidays play a large part in these adventures though they no longer tend to be the prissy romances of old. Phyllis, a lady the Americans would call a 'free spirit,' was roaming round the world on her own when she alighted on Ibiza in the Mediterranean. At a disco she was dancing without her shoes, and when she returned to her table there was a note in the shoe inviting her for a drink. 'There were these two blokes, very rich, with a yacht, a white Alfa Romeo, the lot. Not bad looking, but too old for me. They asked me to ferry their car over to Majorca the following day, and just as I was setting off they asked me if I would mind escorting one of their sons. He was sixteen and reminded me of the boy in *The Catcher in the Rye*, knocking on my cabin door every few minutes with every excuse in the book. When we got to the Yacht Club, there was only one room available ! I had a screen organised and we sailed out for dinner. . . . Daddy had given him wads of money with the instructions that I was to be thoroughly looked after. Well, I think he misread Daddy's instructions. Sure we had pots of champagne and a good dinner and went dancing, but when we got back and I had retired with dignity to my side of the screen he clambered in with me and that was that. I thought it wiser not to wait for Daddy in the morning and got the next boat out!'

Ibiza starred in Michelle Moreau's life too. She is the lovely, voluptuous, dark-curly-haired sister of Jeanne Moreau. And loves young men. 'They are so spontaneous, they don't care where they make love, just inside the front door, on the stairs, even the airing cupboard isn't safe, it's Christmas all the time. At the beginning of an affair I sometimes wonder if they are going to kill themselves with enthusiasm.

'An older woman to a young man is a feast, physically and mentally. I think these affairs are part of a woman's personal growth but to use them just for reassurance against fears of age is very dangerous. Also, an older woman can relieve a man of the sole responsibility of making the sexual overtures. Because she has the confidence to reach out for him, put her hand on his balls, let him know she is not wearing knickers, he can forget his anxieties and fears of rejection. She knows that her sex appeal is not dependent on keeping her mascara straight in bed, will not be ruined if she lets out the occasional fart; a woman's understanding has gone further into sensuality and he can respond to the quality of abandon.'

Lest it should appear that our society is about to be taken over by a monstrous regiment of women whose chief interest is to turn men into sex objects let me assure the world that all the women interviewed agreed that this

43

would be demeaning to both parties. Mutual sexual exploitation is all very well for one night stands, and great fun they can be, but for both the young men and the women there is much to be gained mentally also.

Michelle continues: 'Through my young lovers, particularly my first, I was finally able to find out the person I really was. I could live out my natural *jeunesse*, I didn't have to censure myself. In marriage I had backed down, conformed to the conventional idea of marriage. I had actually imposed these ideas on myself, because that was the thinking of the time when *I* was twenty. We were conditioned to ignore our own sexuality and look for security for the future.

'My lover was very *avante-garde* and he expanded my ideas; it was very liberating. When I was young, women did not admit to the pleasures of lying in bed with a beautiful body; now if I see a man in the street that I want I will turn round and look at him . . . looks, tight jeans and high boots can really turn me on, I don't have to hide that now. Men of my own age are not into the music, books and thinking that interests me.'

Gloria – the deserted American wife of my first Chapter – when I met her, was spending ten days away from home on a flute-playing course. Bill, her young lover, was looking after her teenage kids. 'He has encouraged me to fulfil myself in a way I never allowed myself to do when I was married because of my husband's total lack of interest. A young lover is a very renewing event in one's life, not just the strong young body that is a pleasure to feel and look at across a room, and the happily straightforward sex, but the chance of a fresh look at the world through much younger eyes. In exchange one can provide a background that makes them mature quickly . . . if they are intelligent that is – which of course we think they must be if they have chosen us !'

That fresh look at life is one of the big separating factors between the women who are prepared to take risks, who chance social rebuttal, and those who creep home nightly to a diet of romantic novels, the telly and dreams of a nice, *suitable* second marriage.

Through contact with younger men a woman can explore ignored, undeveloped aspects of her own personality and interests. A young lover sees a woman differently from the friends of her own age, and very differently from her children's view however much nearer their age he may be. He sees a complete woman but not a finished one, and albeit through selfishness, naïvety or just plain, youthful enthusiasm, imposes his interests, opinions and friends on her. Young men haven't yet learned the use of the word 'can't' and neither will their women while they are around.

Mala, a life-enhancing woman if ever I have known one, has had many affairs with young men over the last twelve or so years. She has been married three times, has a grown up son, wears outrageously ethnic clothes and has a smile and heart that would not shame Louis Armstrong. She is forty-seven and never lies about her age. 'I put it out as a statement, if it matters don't come near, to lie would beggar the whole reason, luckily a lot of chaps quite get off on it. My lovers have done a hell of a lot for me, they have kept me in there with youth, stopped me getting into a middle-aged state of mind, stopped me thinking about age, and have taught me that desirability and availability are all you need to have. I think intellectually they come off better out of the relationship, I find their innocence very touching and it's fun to teach them graciousness. I'm not into using young men for sneaky fucks, I know everything starts with a one night stand but I like a relationship to last at least six months. Of course that can bring problems if they get too comfortable; my very first venture into youth was with a beautiful black boy seventeen years my junior and although the sex was very superior to that of my own age-group lovers I didn't want the responsibility. I have no regrets, I sent him on his way wiser, richer (not financially, you understand) and able to grace someone else's life. With another young lover, a Hebridean fisherman, I have seen the Aurora Borealis and learned about nature, living in a croft on the islands; and a young teacher of maths taught me calculus.

'When I was approaching forty I was definitely heading for Grand Dame, tending to pay people to do things for me. I have friends who are positively senile through that, all middle-class and closed minds. But during the last ten years I've been checking everything out through my lovers. Sure I've tried "tripping", pot, speed, even their bloody religions, and I love to listen to them; actually found myself one night being given the most amazing seeing-to by a cottage-queen who had spent hours fascinating me with all the details of why he hangs round men's lavatories, well you don't spend that sort of a day sitting alone in your room do you?

'It's true I have been over-bold, over-hip (my God there's a couple of puns) but I have been learning all the time. I noticed over and over again that I was still carrying the opinions and prejudices of my working-class childhood. Now they have all been banished and my motto, as

I hurtle towards fifty, is *Constant Change is Here to Stay!*'

Luckily Mala has neither the time nor the inclination to embroider such a splendid motto in cross-stitch to frame and hang over her bed; also she has too much tact, but tattooed in the head it could be a lifeline for the bad days.

There is always something to be gained; it may be learning about real ale or fine wines, exploring the occult or the exhilaration of riding pillion on powerful motorbikes, discovering a different kind of music, politics, religion, or, simply to relish a variety of companions. A woman who is willing to try anything, even risking looking foolish in the attempt, usually finds she is not the fool she thought she might be. She can make her life a refresher course in fun and turn her new status as a lone, grown woman into a positive asset that allows her to wander through the generations as it suits her.

Louise looks like a Toulouse-Lautrec portrait, silky grey hair piled into a high chignon, arrogantly carved cheekbones, heavy lidded eyes and a dark lipsticked mouth that can purse over the price of meat or laugh like a girl. When at the age of forty-two she took her son's twenty-one-year-old tutor for a lover she blew the myth on French forbearance; her bourgeois friends were not amused. Twenty-five years later and living now with a young man of thirty-three, *she* still is. 'I really don't like to be with people my own age, except perhaps some women friends, but men in their fifties who have become successful are overbearing, have no generosity of spirit and think they are always right. And, of course, they are often impotent . . . and so dull! They don't laugh much, somehow women always seem to have something fresh, and are gay in themselves.

47

To live with young men is not only good for sex but for atmosphere, they are so full of life, it is never monotonous. I think it is a cliché that older women teach young men how to behave in bed. It is the older men who want a little of this, a little of that. Young men do just what they like, they get on with it. I never ask, just enjoy what I get. Young men are so natural, fresh, I love their naïvety. Also from them I have learnt to jump from one generation to another, to understand and follow their minds, to realize how they live. I stay young in my brain though I carry the imprint of my own generation.

'For instance . . . if I think of my ex-husband! Do you know he has never been out of France? He is wealthy, we had a large house, an estate, horses – but he has never been anywhere. My first love, my young boy, took me travelling, all over America and Mexico, he taught me the value of charter flights and small hotels, now I can live on lots or little and have travelled cheaply all round the world. I met Michael (the young man she has lived with for the past eight years) on a beach in Mykonos, we both had very little money but a lot of fun. He returned to America and I to London but a few months later he was back and we have been together ever since. We have worked together running a nightclub and our life is full of care and companionship.

'The best thing to come out of my life, which has not been all easy, happened to me recently. My son, who was brought up by his father and had a conventional, successful career and marriage, was suddenly divorced. His whole life structure was broken and he needed to get away. I took him to the Greek Islands which I know, we had to queue for tiny charter flights, stay in small inns, travel in cargo boats. He was thirty-five and had only travelled first class before, and through my experience I was able to open his eyes to another world.'

Being able to give both sexually and mentally is another of the advantages of becoming a mature woman. By learning to accept, live with, and laugh at her own shortcomings and faults, a woman slowly grows to expect less of others. She has given up setting standards of excellence for herself, her friends and her lovers, and everyone around her can relax. Gone forever are those agonies of youth when she took a magnifying glass to each minute flaw, enlarged it and promptly felt unworthy of love. She can now feel capable of receiving love from many sources : friendship, casual admiration, affection or straightforward sexual encounter are all easily absorbed. She no longer even wants one man to be all things to her. She needs variety in her life, sometimes in bed, sometimes out of it.

The beauty of a woman in mid-life comes from her joy in herself as she is now; the body may be a bit battered but the spirit is stronger. If she feels she needs a face-lift, or her hair tinted, or expensive beauty care in order to develop her potentialities as a woman, that is her business. The important thing is to not envy her own past youthfulness, nor that of those around her, but to get on with life and enjoy it to the full.

If a woman wishes to be generous with her body, that is her own business, it is her one true possession, God given, as the Bible affirms. She takes from her lovers, certainly . . . but there is an exquisite art in being selfish. Take only what he can give; never demand the impossible; be prepared to move on when the relationship is no longer beneficial. And always try to send a man on his way with his ego intact – ex-lovers make marvellous friends and can be an investment against future loneliness, or, better still, a supply line to other adventures.

The advantages of associations with younger men can stimulate a woman's career, too. A grown woman acknowledging that she still has much to learn, that mistakes are something to be overcome, not to be overwhelmed by, is a confident person, aware of the possibilities of the future, her horizons unlimited.

Molly Parkin is a tailor-made example. 'Patrick encouraged me to stretch my talents, he taught me to be adventurous, to aim higher, whereas all the other men I had been with, my three resident lovers, thought I had done terribly well to reach *The Sunday Times*. To them it was an Establishment thing, a safe harbour you reach in middle age and stay in until you can retire with dignity.

'Patrick is the one who pushed me on and said try something else – made me write all this filth!!' She added archly, 'I couldn't possibly write what I write now if I were on my own because it makes me too vulnerable. As it is we have had to take my name out of the telephone book. I met him at the perfect time in my career, just two weeks after joining *The Sunday Times* when I couldn't even write a caption. He helped me enormously.'

Help goes both ways and Patrick, too, has grown into his own gifts with Molly's understanding that the necessity to teach is death to art.

Shirley Young – one of London's fashion world's leading PRs – and her young man Barry have nutured each other's business talents with sympathetic support in times of stress. Says Shirley, 'We have tremendous pride in each other, if I have a success he is terribly proud and if I ever have a failure he always blames the other person. I think that's one of his endearing qualities because what you don't need when you are down is your partner saying "I told you so." ' Shirley and Barry have proved their point by their mutual success, and have a beautiful house in acres of their own ground.

A lot of couples seem to meet through work – yet another incentive to get out into the world. Joan Bakewell, whose story is related on page 54, met her young husband Jack Emery when she went to interview him for a television programme. He too has encouraged her aspirations to be a writer.

It must be understood that here we have been talking about couples and women with very individual careers. But there will be many women in all walks of life in the transition period whose relationships with younger men will be perhaps strictly for fun value – and there is a risk that these relationships can affect a career adversely. A woman with a job in an office or shop who arrives late for work exhausted from drinking, dancing or screwing all night may find herself out of favour with the boss. *He* is likely to be about the same age as herself and may well view the sparkle in her eye with a very jaundiced one of his own. Tolerant of the ways of youngsters in his charge because being happy is associated with youth in his mind, he will almost certainly disapprove of a woman of his own age enjoying a life-style that his family and mortgage have curtailed for him. And he is more than likely to feel threatened in some vague macho corner of his being if he suspects that the source of her sparkle is a team of young men.

However many the temptations, and I hope there are hundreds, business and sex life must be kept separate if one is to get the benefit of both.

Talking of the advantages of affairs with younger men

most women agreed that, once you were really into it, the mental freedom of not thinking in numbers, like age, was reflected in the clothes they wore. I had a lot of laughs with the women I interviewed about our past attempts to attain perfection. Rueful ones about the rubber roll-ons smelling of talc with which we had confined our youthful bodies. The anxieties of a safety-pinned bra strap, those absurd bee-hive hairdos wired up with an armoury of hairpins and cemented with lacquer. I can actually remember thinking that I was too old for tights when they first came on the market about fifteen years or so ago – I thought they were strictly for the young! And sadly I heard only the other day a pretty, well-preserved woman in her early fifties declare that she couldn't buy a pair of boots in case the people in her office thought she was trying to look like a dolly bird.

Fashion is supposed to reflect society and in recent years the range and variety of options have grown immensely as women have learned to suit themselves and dress according to their mood of the day. The age barrier has practically disappeared from the clothes racks in the shops, a woman can wear jeans and a sloppy sweater one day, satin and pearls the next if she wants to. It was interesting to note that most of the women with younger lovers adopt a kind of sophisticated, casual look that bridges the generation gap without attempting to look competitive. Also, their self-assurance makes them much less vain; it is not the older ones you see in the ladies' loos desperately re-painting, brush stroke by brush stroke, another layer of artificial perfection on their faces. They have learned that their attractions rely more on what goes on inside the head (and of course, the bed), chiefly because they have had to. No amount of make-up can hide the beauty of a young woman's skin and one of the reasons the older woman doesn't linger in the loo too long is that she has learned the sense not to allow comparisons into her mind lest they should be too demoralising. We have to guard our inner sense of security . . . like Fort Knox.

Curiously I have almost neglected to mention one of the most unexpected discoveries of my research – that amongst all the chat about the lustiness of young men there emerged the fact that they are also very romantic.

Any woman of any age is a sucker for the romantic gesture, but one who has been through the hell of rejection and the sense of failure that instils itself like a creeping fog towards the end of a marriage is very susceptible to sweetness and gentle kindness. Being wooed again is wonderful; simple thoughtfulness like a phone call in the middle of the day with nothing to say except 'hello,' like making sure you have enough of your brand of cigarettes, giving you a paperback he thinks you might like to read, wearing a tie because he knows it will please you, all these are utterly endearing acts that make a woman feel deliciously desirable again. Sure, some of them are only interested in getting their end away – nothing wrong with that if it's a two-way enthusiasm – but there are many, many more who offer tenderness and admiration along with their lust.

One woman I met had gone through a particularly hideous operation. She had known for three months that she must have a colostomy and during that time she met a very beautiful young man and decided to have a last fling before her body was defiled (in her eyes) for ever. Before she went into hospital she told him the truth and that he must now go on his way. A month later she was back home recuperating, very depressed and trying to adjust to the idea that her sex life was over. At that moment her young man appeared at her window, he had climbed up the outside of her house to assure her that the operation would not make any difference to his desire for her – and promptly proved it. The affair did not last but her morale was restored and she still attracts many young lovers.

When Jack Emery met Joan Bakewell she had just been pole-axed by the end of a relationship, 'walking wounded' was how she described herself. And although she had earmarked Jack as a very nice young man who might do as an escort she had no intention of embarking on a new affair, particularly with someone ten years her junior. 'He was simply lodged in my mind as an available man, I knew his marriage had just collapsed so when he offered me a platonic week-end in Cornwall it didn't seem at all extraordinary and I accepted. Then he arrived to pick me up in an E-type Jag. filled with Fortnum's-style groceries, champagne and flowers – I thought it was terrifically romantic but still I was aware that I was older and had a lot of experience, and I was quite convinced that he would be naïve in contrast. The discovery that he wasn't made all the difference.

'On the Monday morning he put me on the train and filled my arms with daffodils but I read the riot act to him and told him that he was not to fall in love with me. I said we had had a good time but I didn't want it to develop, I was going off to Malta with my children, and he promptly stated that he didn't mind about the children and would fly over for the week-end.'

Jack arrived in the middle of the night bearing a bottle of cold champagne and scent which he thought was the style to which she was accustomed. Her journey to Malta had been a hairy one, with one of the plane's engines failing, and on the way she had promised herself 'if I survive this I'm going to marry him.'

So Joan had already made up her mind and when Jack said, several bottles of champagne later, 'I have something to ask you' she answered 'yes' . . . he never had the chance to pop the actual question.

One of the sweetest, most lovingly romantic stories happened to *me* at Christmas . . . I awoke to find a Christmas sock (a rather battered navy-blue one) complete with silver-wrapped tangerine, an apple, nuts and sweeties, and my present in the toe, hanging from my bedside table. Oh, the contrast to the many years of slaving over turkey-filled ovens, cursing brandy butter, separating squabbling siblings! We sat up in bed and drank Buck's Fizz, played Scrabble and listened to the carol services on the radio, it was a chance to be a child again. My children were each spending their Christmas happily amongst their own friends and I was free to be given yet another day to remember forever.

Calculating women, the ones who expect to end a weekend in bed with a Monday morning trip to Cartiers, are seldom interested in young men, so Jane, a widow, was quite unprepared for a devastating gesture from her young lover, her first venture into youth, whom she met soon after she was widowed. He was a merchant banker, Hans. The affair was a very happy one, and had been flourishing a couple of months when one day, seated at her desk in her office, she received a phone call from him. 'I'm in Cartiers in Geneva and they have this new love ring, what is your finger size?' It was not the sort of question she was used to answering and she had to run round the office to find a tape measure. 'It was funny really,' said Jane, 'I had never met a man like him before, he could not understand, he

55

took it for granted that every woman knew her ring size. But he came back with the ring and it fitted perfectly. I asked him how he had done it and he told me that he had lined up every female assistant in Cartiers until he found a hand that looked and felt like mine.'

Of course romance doesn't always last but, like good manners and courtesy to another human being, it is an addition to life. Jane's affair ended when the gifts became too many and too formal, the imagination had gone and she knew he had found someone else, but she had enjoyed the year with him so nothing was really lost.

For most of us, the chances are we will have to make do with gestures of the heart, or better still, the cock.

To Gloria, the fact that her young man organises her children to clean up after themselves and take the pressure off her, that is romance.

To Lynda, a cartoon illustrating her new water-tank that sounded as if it had Jacques Cousteau installed in it . . . little notes and rude drawings left round the flat are one of my favourite compliments, too.

There are many ways a young man makes his love felt apart from his refusal to take no for an answer; one woman's eyes got very moist as she recalled the day her young lover lent her son his best clothes and accompanied them both to the juvenile court.

Romance can be being lifted bodily over a puddle in the road or finding a young man sitting outside your front door waiting in the pouring rain for you to come home. It can be that classic gesture of putting his jacket round your shoulders when the weather turns unexpectedly cold or remembering to bring a screwdriver to mend a broken plug.

Gifts don't have to cost money to be deeply touching –

a pebble from the beach shows he was thinking of you, so does making the bed if you have to leave first or smiling across the room if a pretty girl is chatting him up. Shared laughter is romantic, too, and young men have the happy ability to take disaster in their stride. Non-appearing buses, a ghastly waiter on the one day he has the money to take you to dinner, or keeping cavey while you have a desperate piddle in an alleyway – all events that would make an older man fume – are just silly, funny happenings to them. The important thing is that they are with you.

Romance and love do not necessarily go together any-more than lust and love do but they do make a marvellous difference to life until the real thing comes along. And any memories that bring back a twinkle to the eye or a blush to the cheek are as comforting as money in the bank – just in case the real thing doesn't.

Looking through these pages of anecdotes I am now thoroughly convinced that the chief advantage of the older woman's relationships with younger men is, in fact – her age! She is old enough to appreciate everything that happens to her and bold enough to let it happen. She has completed the first half of her adventure through life; she has survived raising a family or accepted that she will never have one, she probably has a broken marriage or unful-filled hopes behind her. Either way she should be able to embark on the second half of her life with the knowledge that the hardest part, the long haul to some semblance of maturity, is over. Alas, this broad rule cannot apply to all women; some will be burdened with the sickness of others and some by their own timidity, but I assume that those of you who read this book are somewhere along, and seek-ing, the road to personal freedom.

Of course you are entitled to dither a bit, consider your own set of circumstances, strengths and weaknesses. You are old enough to think for yourselves. But for those who *do* take the deep breath, decide that the next twenty or thirty years are their own, and can cast off the idea of age being a disgrace, there is so much fun and adventure ahead. And so many, many young men out there who would like to help you find it.

For women in, or approaching, their forties there are sexual pleasures that were practically taboo in our youth. Why not take them? You can always explain to yourself that it is purely medicinal. You are keeping your body healthy and fit, and saving the N.H.S. a fortune on prescribed tranquillisers! You can forgive yourself the hypocrisy as soon as you really begin to enjoy your new life.

Then there are the social pleasures – the new faces, places, interests in your life. All those things made possible by the confidence given to you, and joyously taken by you, from the young men in your life.

And then there is the pleasure of self-fulfilment, the chance to start again through new, possibly varied, partners. The idea of independence and the need for the encouragement and attention of young lovers is not a paradox; we are all human beings with something to learn, something to give, something to take.

It's a fair swop!

3

THE PROBLEMS

The pleasures of associating with men younger than one-self are numerous, there is so much to be gained; sex, warmth, growth, but it would be foolish to deny that barging through the age barrier with a bang, so to speak, has its own problems. As only a fool enters a minefield without first studying any available map so the woman moving out of the security of her entrenched life needs as much information of the dangers ahead as is obtainable.

Young men can be stimulating, undependable, lively, selfish, ardent and casual. And while they solve one set of fears, that of loneliness, of loss of femaleness, of not-belonging, they, being human and young, cannot help providing the occasional disappointment and pain. That's Life – so this chapter must be in the nature of a Cautionary Tale in parts. It is up to each woman to assess for herself whether she can take the odd set-back; in my experience most women with a strong sexual drive can and do.

It is certainly not easy for the woman without the confidence bestowed by a career or a satisfying job to have a second go at life, particularly as she has probably been looking for signs of age since she was thirty. Also if she has spent years neglecting herself, sublimating her sexual urge in a plethora of cream buns, it is even more difficult to rethink herself into being a nice piece of crumpet. But it can be done. As we have seen in Chapter One, the turning point changes the direction of a woman's life, taking her onward at a time when she could atrophy into premature old age.

At first she may re-live adolescent mistakes; waiting in for a telephone call, building too much on a casual liaison, she may feel guilty, embarrassed, over-aware of other people's reactions, easily slighted – her re-kindled sexual fire can lead her into all sorts of scrapes. There is much to be learnt and adjusted to, and a sense of humour is essential now; if she laughs at herself no one can jeer at her. As Gloria says, 'If you've been through the holocaust it also means that you are no longer so giving to the point of defencelessness as you were when young. I think it takes about five years to get over a bad marriage break-up and by then one is ready.'

One of the reasons the older woman no longer gives to the point of defencelessness is that she has learned the hard way that nobody wants it. When one is young one truly believes that one's heart, and indeed one's life, belong entirely to another – and what one wants is theirs in return. Young love is demanding, obsessive, draining, a fine festering ground for jealousy, imagined slights and all the destructive forces that go with such passion. A woman has learned, often through the lesson of letting her children, or, painfully, her husband, go . . . that other people must have their own space. If she is sensible she has also learned to need and enjoy her own, and is as Gloria says, ready.

Ready or not, self-doubt is usually the first problem she encounters as even the fruity Mala admits. 'I did regard him with a certain amount of suspicion at first. I kept thinking, what on earth could he see in me? What was he after, was it money? I thought about it a lot afterwards and found I had no feelings of guilt, I was actually very flattered, I honestly felt a bit triumphant and suddenly realised there was a whole new stratum of desirable opportunities ahead of me.'

Amongst the women who had suffered doubts I found that most of the guilty feelings occurred before the act rather than after, though I still think that in the early stages of transition it is sensible not to enquire too closely about men's ages. Mental arithmetic is one of the assets a woman can well do without when embarking on a career as a *femme fatale*.

Some of the problems are quite comical, particularly in hindsight. Clothes for instance, few young men can either afford or want to dress to match the standards of a woman in her forties.

Nine years ago when Molly Parkin first met Patrick she had just become the fashion editor of *The Sunday Times*. 'I was terribly chic in my Elizabeth Taylor black mink coat and he was in jeans and torn black T-shirts as became a painter. When we were walking along the road together I felt terribly embarrassed, there was this ghastly disparity in our appearance which I felt emphasised our age difference. I wanted to shelve the black mink and climb into jeans but women like me weren't going around in jeans then, there wasn't any way I could dress in the same manner as him. I tried to de-glamourise myself, which was a mistake because that was what he liked about me, my exotic image, he was proud of the way I looked.

'I suppose there are two sorts of younger men, there are *The Roman Spring of Mrs Stone* kind, the well-dressed gigolo and . . . ("A bit of rough trade?" prompted Patrick) yes, well of all the women I know who have gone with younger men, none of the fellas are posh. But then I started using Patrick as my dolly, I liked to dress him up. Now he looks like a well-dressed gigolo !'

It was an exchange that brought forth groans of agreement from me. I remember feeling quite obscenely antique in my hard fought for, brand-new red fox being escorted by my even newer lover in his skin-tight jeans and leather bomber jacket. To make matters worse he was shorter than I in my teetering high heels, added to which he looked about sixteen although he was thirty-three. One day my temper snapped and I insisted that he changed into a suit, this he did with such amiable acquiescence that I finally learnt the art of compromise. I now wear jeans, my figure having improved under his constant attentions, and *his* shirts and bomber jacket.

Niké Williams ran into the opposite situation, she wanting to go around in the lackadaisical fashions she portrays in *Honey* magazine – khaki fatigues and ballooning trousers gathered in over ankle socks and kiddy sandals; 'But they wanted the full Marilyn Monroe image, slit skirts and cleavage. I used to feel terribly self-conscious going to the theatre or restaurants, thinking everybody must be pointing at us and saying how ridiculous; that young boy out with her ! But after a while I realised that happiness had made me look ten years younger and people were only saying "what an attractive couple." '

Less comical, indeed truly nerve-wracking at first, is the state of one's body at the age of forty-five or so. Although the tide is changing now, and character and personality in women are beginning to be both respected and admired, youthful perfection has for so long been the standard of desirability that it is not surprising that the older woman is forced to feel inadequate. Child-bearing hips, drooping tits, stretch marks, how could any young man with his firm frame and satiny skin want all that?

The answer is simple and coarse. It is the two bits that surround the hips, tits and stretch marks that interest him. The head, with its face full of character and warmth, and the uninhibited, unpossessive cunt. These are the qualities that the older woman has to offer and as long as she realises they are positive qualities, not in any way to be confused with what she had to offer twenty years ago, she need not make a fool of herself but can add to her own life and to that of the people she meets.

In my time I have listened to too many cheerfully cruel conversations between young men about women who have looked 'nine pints beautiful' the night before ever to risk them finding me *au naturel* on the pillow in the morning. I *know* what I look like in the morning after a good night's drinking, dancing and screwing, and it's not an experience I wish to share. Sneaking out of bed so as not to disturb the supine incumbent and hot-footing it to the bathroom where a glamorous robe and a brand new face can be applied seems to be both sensible and courteous. Not too much of a shock for the poor little bugger as you bring him a cup of tea – and the chance of his early morning sunrise.

Should the relationship develop into real intimacy then these ploys become redundant, time spent together exploring each other's personality lends itself to honesty and a form of love, however temporary.

Again, the forthright Molly: 'I felt desperately self-conscious of my body with Patrick. I was still going to bed with my other men, who are in my age group, and getting undressed in the corner. I was shy. I had always been shy, I was brought up to be shy and it was Patrick who taught me to undress with the light on. I was also very self-conscious of my stretch marks from the children of my first marriage.'

At that moment the irrepressible Patrick mumbles in the background : 'Ah, but they are quite remarkable really, like the Sierra Nevada.'

That's enough to make or break a relationship if ever I heard one.

But Molly agrees. 'Mmm, yes, sort of saggy stomach — nobody had ever mentioned it before, but you twanged on it, didn't you? Actually somebody had noticed it before and suggested I wear a roll-on in bed ... just what you need! But I did feel it to be a terrible contrast with his young body.'

This praise for the beauty of young men's bodies ran like a chorus through all the conversations with women : 'their strong young bodies that are a pleasure to feel and look at across a room'; 'their shape, their skin'; 'just to look at him naked turns me on'; were the average reactions. There is no shame in the joy of beauty. It is this joy that makes the same women actively repelled by men of their own age : 'they want to tell you their troubles, make excuses before they even get you into bed'; 'they can't get it up'; 'they grope'; 'there are even men with great big dongs who have never learned to make love'; was the general consensus of opinion.

'And they do not look after their bodies the way women do now' was the chief complaint. Women do at least try, though not all attain the standards of Gillian Bobroff, who is forty, and married to her third husband, David, who is thirty. Gillian is a woman who has lived more lives than most young men have eaten hot dinners. She owns a successful model agency and has a figure to compete with the girls half her age. She works at it, getting up at 6 a.m. for exercises, massage and swimming several times a week, then on to a formidable day's work in the office and out on the town whenever she can manage it. With her bright, blonde good looks and the opportunities concomitant with her career she is an expert at dealing with young men (she eloped with her second husband when he was nineteen). 'Today I've learned that there are two kinds of behaviour . . . my husband's and mine. He has had to learn that it does not enhance my career if for example he gets up halfway through a boring business dinner and speaks his mind. The only way to deal with it is to explain your point of view the following day; that you might look a fool.

'On my part I try not to be possessive. I try not to hit him over the head with a coat-hanger when I see him talking to another girl, and in fact he is always very quick to state our relationship. I like that feeling of his caring.'

Gillian had put her finger on two of the outstanding problems between older women and younger men, both of them feeding off basic insecurities. A young man's fears of inadequacy, not as a sexual partner but as a man, his unknowingness of the ways of the world; and the older woman's fear of losing him to a younger woman.

If a woman flaunts her young man as a stud, especially in front of her own age group, he is more than likely to go on the turn, drink too much, and display his contempt for the older generation, her friends, in no uncertain terms. Even though it is unfair that a husband can get pissed as a fart and be carried out by the head-waiter without the slightest embarrassment to his wife, the fact remains that a young lover is a reflection of his woman. It is shrewder to keep business and love lives well separated, at least in the early stages of the affair. The ground is very unobliging about opening up and swallowing her as the boyfriend gropes the boss's wife's bum or falls asleep in his steak tournedos.

Few of us have the aplomb of Dorothy Parker in such a situation. She once took one of her many pretty young men to a very distinguished dinner party and the poor chap's nerve broke when he was ushered into this den of literary lions. He took to the martinis and was drunk by the time they got to the table. The meal had barely started before he got up announcing loudly 'I wanna piss,' and staggered from the room. 'He's very shy,' said the unperturbed Ms Parker, 'actually he only wants to telephone.'

Most young men are very sweet about not preying on jealousy, they are attentive about lighting cigarettes and filling glasses – and if they *are* out to make waves they are frankly not worth your time of night. They are, in fact, dangerous to a woman's equilibrium, as Harriet – twice-married and divorced, cultured and elegant and forty-nine – found out when she fell passionately in love with a man of thirty-one. 'He destroyed me,' she says simply, 'he lied to me, deceived me and was brutal. He taught me the danger of having your wishes granted. He was everything sexually, but that was because I was in love. We had violent rows and he would scream at me that I didn't love him, I just wanted him because he was the best fuck I had ever had. That was partly true because as you get older you are not going to have a relationship with someone who doesn't satisfy you sexually. When you are younger your love is much more pure, you love them "because", but as you get older you want sex.

'The real horror began when I discovered he was married. I had had affairs with two married men before, both when their marriages were in a state of crisis, and had sworn to myself Never Again. So when I met Keith (and he was *so beautiful*) and he followed me to a restaurant to ask my telephone number, I asked him straight away if he was married or shacked up with anyone. He told me "no," so when he rang I was astonished and delighted, but of course he was lying.

'To my eternal shame I shopped him to his wife when I found out the truth, and this broke up his marriage. She was young and expecting a child. It was horrible, but still I couldn't resist him. I knew there were other women but each time he came back into my life, I couldn't help myself, he had such magnetism, I accepted all the humiliations.

'Through him I lost the last remnants of my youth, and all I gained in exchange was knowledge of a set of cruelties I had never encountered before. The bags under my eyes are forever a memorial to him, they belong to him. He has taken my resilience from me.'

Harriet volunteered this information when she heard me discussing the title of this book; she was right to point out that there are many pitfalls, that an overpowering sexual urge can lead to a sacrifice of self-respect, but perhaps wrong to blame her painful experience on the age difference. There is always the risk that whichever man you choose, whatever shape, size, colour, creed or age, he may turn out to be a shit. I have been there myself, notably with a young, entertaining charmer who made me laugh all the time . . . right up to the moment he rang me to cancel a date when his wife had been taken to hospital because the baby looked as if it was going to be born three weeks early.

I felt hideous, I wouldn't have done that to any woman in the world. He felt quite guiltless. "Oh, I thought you knew," was his only comment. Luckily I had other lovers to fall back on, I had not been obsessed by him, just adored his company. It proved to me a point with which many grown women agree; that unless you are actually living with someone, there is safety in numbers. If you have a team of young lovers you are not likely to worry too much about what they are doing when they are not with you. This is not promiscuity, just good sense. It helps the older woman to put a rein on potential possessiveness, to make use of the lessons learned from the past; of letting offspring go, of not lamenting the passing of homes, good times, friends. Of course other women are going to fancy your man, other men too these days, he would be boring otherwise. You have to be realistic and recognise that one day circumstances or choice will move either one of you on. Which makes it all the sillier to ruin the good times with petty jealousy.

It is the women who have had several long-staying relationships with younger lovers that fear young girls the least. Louise can watch the girls flirting with her tall, handsome Texan with amusement. 'I know they don't interest him and he always behaves impeccably to me, but as you grow older your feelings grow less strong, you have not so much energy to waste on jealousy.'

And it never occurs to Molly Parkin. As she gets older she is determined to become more exotic, like Mae West, Colette or Edith Piaf.

Erica has found living with and travelling round the world with Graham, ten years her junior, a complete antidote to jealousy. 'I no longer live in fear as I did with my ex, I had been agonisingly jealous and it was all his fault because he *made* me aware of what he was doing; always a little mistake or those slight, secret looks between two people that you are not supposed to miss. The funny thing is I didn't do half the things with him that I do with Graham, like scream and shout and behave badly – I suppose I am more confident now.'

After that conversation we had a wicked little thought. Might not our penchant for young men lead us to discard *them* as they grew older? There's a thought to keep them on their toes!

Money must figure in the list of problems. Once again a perfectly acceptable state of affairs between a younger woman and an older man, his power and his money add to his charisma. Admittedly no man can be called a fortune-hunter in these days of high taxation but the less than posh bloke is certainly viewed with narrowed eyes as he moves in on the life-style of a successful lady of middle years. Not least by her.

Finance was one of the few areas I found while researching this book where women were prepared to be less than honest. Whilst willing to own up to the pleasures of the reversing of a traditional situation they were unwilling to accept that they may be paying the same price as older men. Whereas a man is delighted to bestow expensive presents on his child-bride and happy to pay for everything, a similar admission from women was given with great reluctance. They have a million excuses to explain away the fact that their young men are living off them.

'I make him do the household chores to earn his drinking money,' was one; 'I want him to concentrate on his musical talents,' was another; 'I would have to pay the rent if I was living alone,' yet another. None of the women

I met were into giving sapphire cuff-links but many were anxious to disregard the fact that they paid all the bills; for food, for his laundry, cleaning and the occasional shirt or pair of trousers because, 'I like him to look nice when he comes out with me.'

Going 'Dutch' when out is acceptable in all age groups but a living-in circumstance is much trickier. I tried it once and it was a disaster for both of us. He stayed at home working on a project that was to make our fortunes while I went out to work. He ended up feeling less than a man and becoming sexually unresponsive, I stayed out with the boys, coming home later and later to complaints that my dinner was spoiled. Women are amenable creatures but not to the point where they despise their man. Compromise is important here, so perhaps the little white lies, the excuses, are forgivable.

In any case a woman who has moved up in the world by her own efforts has become acclimatised to a certain standard of living. Expense account lunches, taxis everywhere, receptions, previews, first nights and so on are part of some successful women's scene. They are used to paying their own way when necessary – but also used to being cossetted. Women are well known for their adaptability, but changing from champagne at the Ritz to half a pint of bitter at the local for the sake of a young lover's ego and pocket – perhaps good fun at first – can be depressing, disorientating, and downright destructive to the delicate buds of lust in the long term. Giving the young lover money to buy the drinks either in private or public may be worse – smacking of buying his services. But as quotable Mala says, 'few young men have the money to keep me tanked up, so in bars I just leave the money on the table and we take it in turn to order, nobody really notices. Restaurants are cool, after all you do it with your own age group, so why not?'

Eva, whom I interviewed over the same problem, agrees. 'If you are going to maintain your own life-style then you have to expect to pick up the tab, so long as you don't take it as a sign that they are used to living off the welfare, as it were. It's a matter of tact. But sending them up to the bar with a £10 note is humiliating for them. You really must treat them socially as you would a girlfriend – that is very important. And of course you can always offer them money as a *loan*. You may never get it back but then you often don't from friends.'

But in a long term affair the inequality of bank balance can, and does, cause resentment on both sides. Molly Parkin and Patrick had to cope with this situation, mostly because Patrick had to support his ex-wife and three sons. He admits, 'It's very painful, being a man and not paying or paying less than half your share which I did until recently.' 'Yes,' agrees Molly, 'it's very demeaning. And people always think he is with you because you have made the money – that is where the relationship can flounder, over money. I think at the beginning I used to resent it as well and when I got drunk I used to say horrible things. I was desperately sorry the next day because I didn't really feel like that, I'm naturally generous, but something must have been there otherwise it wouldn't have come out when I was drunk. And there are other times when you are in financial difficulties yourself, you think, fucking hell, here I am past forty, scrabbling around for bits of fucking money when I could have been with someone who would give me money for a house or a holiday.'

Erica, too, has been stung by other people's willingness to not mind their own business. 'Graham won't have a bank account and his salary goes into my bank, so when I cash a cheque in a pub and he puts the money into his pocket people go "aagh!" There's no point explaining that it is his money – they don't want to believe it. There is one girl round Soho I will never forgive. I had lent a friend some money which I needed back to buy our flat. The friend gave this girl the money to hand over to me, which she did, saying, "Don't let Graham see any of that or he'll drink it all." Fucking cheek.'

The Oedipus complex is another problem that many women, and indeed their young men, are anxious to deny, and yet the trap is there for both partners. It is easy for a woman who has spent the larger part of her grown-up life looking after children to assume the same role with a young man when her kids have left home. Fortunately the new generation of young men are trained to independence from an early age. They are used to going to the launderette, cooking for themselves, cleaning the bath and doing the washing-up. A lot depends on the man's age, whether he has lived alone and learned self-sufficiency, and a lot on the home circumstances into which he is introduced. Michelle has found on a couple of occasions that she has drifted in to the mothering role. 'The guy becomes part of the family, it is bound to happen if he gets on well with your children. One guy who moved in had all the usual problems, he was twenty-six, I was thirty-eight, he had no money and certainly expected me to be more understanding of his problems because I was older. It was all very one-sided. It depends whether you like it or not, and whether you can give him the answers he is looking for. I did become the mother for a while but at the same time I enjoyed looking after him.'

Erica and Molly both confess to making a conscious

effort to look after their men, making sure that there is always a plentiful supply of good food and clean clothes in the house. Here I have to add that such a role has no appeal for me; when it comes to washing socks and underpants I have an ungenerous soul, and in any case I am a rotten housewife. I did make an attempt when my lover started a new job; each evening I prepared a delicious meal and ran a bath for him when he got home. By the fourth day I would have made a combustion engine look like a dried-out battery. 'I don't want to be a fucking wife,' I screamed. 'And I don't want a fucking mother!' was the welcome answer. We had a drink, a good laugh, and from that day have shared all the chores, or ignored them.

But sometimes choosing a *very* young man forces the role of mother on to the woman whether she welcomes it or not, and invariably she doesn't because it is mother as ogre she finds herself becoming.

Niké expressed regret that she had not taken the chance and married her first beautiful young lover of nineteen and had the baby he wanted, but two of the women I talked to, who had taken the risk, have watched their young lovers grow not into men but into destroyed boys. Both of them were candid, honest women, not at all what the Americans would call 'ball-breakers'; each had fallen in love with a nineteen-year-old when they were in their thirties.

Lois was thirty-nine when she met Peter, she married him because she was pregnant, although she had three children by a previous marriage. She could have tried for an abortion but took the advice of a doctor friend who said, 'Peter will blame you if you abort or if you don't, so make up your mind what you want to do.' She was in love with him

73

and proposed. Lois is now fifty-five and keeping the two children of the marriage on welfare. Peter is thirty-five and has a drink problem that recently landed him in the psychiatric ward. She is a womanly woman with remarkable eyes and great fortitude. And she still loves her Peter.

'He has always loved drink and the company of men. When we were first married I used to run after him, go to the pub and make tremendous scenes, smashing glasses and insisting that he came home. He liked that, it gave him a discipline and he desperately needed to be wanted, he had been thrown out by his adoptive parents for his long hair. But as the children grew older I couldn't leave them to go after him and other men dragged him further into drink.

'Then he would pick rows as an excuse to go to the pub. I genuinely think that young men have emotional homosexual feelings; with Peter, his men friends always came first, he would do anything for them. But when I was ill he was full of resentment, instead of coming to see me at the hospital that I was in for a check-up he rang me to tell me that I had cancer! Worse, it was true.

'I even divorced him after thirteen years to give him his freedom, I thought that was what he wanted, then I found he was living with another older woman and that I couldn't stand. I ran after him again, and now he is back with me. When all is said and done he is the one I want in my bed, it is his skin I want to touch, we may play mother and baby in bed, and because he drinks too much our sex life isn't very frequent, but I know he needs me and to me he will always be a man.'

Phyllis, too, had watched her young husband turn from a sweetheart into a violent drinker. Although the age difference was less – she was thirty-two when she met him – her

74

previous life-style as an actress who had balled every leading man in Hollywood, and as a woman who had floated round the world alone, constituted a threat to him. The marriage lasted ten years and has left her somewhat more than indifferent to the feelings of others, something which she admits is more than likely a safety valve.

'It became impossible, and the longer we lived together the more he felt threatened by my past life. He became obsessively possessive, stifling. I know he tried to keep it under control, and I tried to help, I mean if we were at a party I would always dance with the ugliest man in the room, but still there would be a scene. I suppose the drinking was an attempt to disguise his own sense of inadequacy but there wasn't any need.

'In the end I didn't treat him very well because I didn't like the me I had become. He made me into a mother figure, and a nagging bitch of a mother figure at that, which I didn't want ... I wasn't interested in fucking babies. As soon as I was happy, in the most trivial way like singing around the house, he would engineer a row so that I would become the bullying mother shouting at him for not developing his own talent. He was a very promising pop musician when I met him, pretty and a darling, and at first I looked after the business side of his life. Then he just wanted jobs that gave him drinking money and ignored his talent.

'It was very sad because the first few years were magical, I was so happy being a soft, gentle person. I wanted him to know that he had given these qualities to me, but he couldn't accept the gift. Even my friends saw the change in me but still he thought I would go back to my old ways, that he wouldn't be able to keep me. Finally, of course, I realised he was wasting his life and mine, and we fell into

75

a dreadful pattern ... I got to moaning, nagging all the time, and he took refuge in being dirty and scruffy.

'He has gone back to America now, ostensibly to re-discover his talent, to go back to music, but all I feel is a total sense of release, of freedom – and my new lover is twenty-four, tremendously selfish, but with just that extra inch I need.'

Since the whole point of this book is to learn something about ourselves as women facing the second half of our lives, to enjoy the next twenty years rather than suffer, it would seem advisable to leave the very young to marinate in life a little longer.

Any woman who is not prepared to sit out the years in safety is likely to make some mistakes and it must be faced that there are bound to be incidents that only the distance of time can heal. Inevitably there will be rejections, lame excuses and outright snubs from men who have not yet learned to manage their manners with ease; it isn't inten-tional cruelty, just the awkwardness of youth. It would be very unfair of a grown woman to make him feel uncom-fortable with the flicker of an eye and a half-hidden know-ing smile next time she sees him ... but just occasionally, it is quite irresistible. We all have to live and learn that not all experiences are pleasant.

I had an absolute beaut in Los Angeles; I met this deliriously handsome heterosexual man, a rarity in Cali-fornia. He looked like a cigarette ad and had a brain about the size of a filter tip, but the rest of him was king-sized. He knocked on my door with flattering regularity and one day casually asked me the ages of my children back home. Quandary time. I knew that with my tan and starvation rations (I was writing an uncommissioned book at the time) I could knock quite a few years off but I would be left looking like a prize bitch of a mother deserting her children for her ambitions. Foolishly I opted for the truth, give or take a year or so, and twenty minutes later he was up, dressed and I never saw him again. I have to admit I missed his brain for weeks!

Famous women have no choice about owning up to age, unless they have been very shrewd early on, and quite frankly I seldom believe the women who do, I prefer Louise's outlook : 'I never lie about my age . . . but then, I never tell it either.' Phyllis has decided that the scrapbook of her heyday in Hollywood is safer at the bottom of her wardrobe. There is no point keeping physically fit, mentally alert and sexually vital in order to be admired as a well-preserved ancient monument.

One of the more up-to-date fears that faces the modern woman left single in mid-life is that of being thought, or even of becoming, a lesbian. It is a subject that has been well aired by the Gay Liberation factions of both sexes, and while it has brought freedom to those sexually inclined to their own gender, it could have a sadly inhibiting effect on friendship amongst women at a time when they need it most. Two women sitting in a pub or club, enjoying each other's company, can be easily dismissed as 'a couple of old dykes' if they refuse an offer of a drink from a man they don't wish to talk to. It has happened to my daughter and myself, it even happened to me in print (it gave Fleet Street the laugh of the year and my bank balance a cheering boost in damages) but to women embarking on a new life, alone, uncertain of their sex-appeal, their future, or their own feelings towards the opposite sex, such remarks can be a heavy setback. They have become outsiders, they are no longer half of a couple, have indeed become an unwilling threat to their securely married friends. They need to talk, to share problems, they need company, comfort, a form of love, affection. Does that mean that all this time they have been nuturing secret lesbian tendencies?

'No,' says Glenn Wilson, of the Institute of Psychiatry, very firmly, 'I can't imagine anyone being converted to lesbianism because of lack of male talent being available at the time. If they turned to it in a positively sexual sense it would mean that they had had a predisposition from very much younger. They would have known. More likely two women of similar interest live together because they are not concerned with some distant concept of the future and are simply living for the here and now.'

The idea of women's conscious-raising groups has always been more popular in the States than here, English manners are weaned on reticence, but a woman *friend* can be a life-line; something between 4 a.m. and the whole bottle of tranquillisers, someone to go to a party with, or someone who can, through laughter, turn yesterday's disaster into today's joke.

Gay men are an alternative form of friendship and more women than I had expected have had affairs with bisexual men, usually very warm and worldly women who, through understanding their own sensuality could accept it in another; the men, unencumbered by a sense of macho, were free to proffer a relationship both tender and sexual.

Glenn Wilson is convinced through his research that the male bisexual has a very strong libido, which would, of course, make him a satisfactory physical lover to a woman who has reached a high sexual peak herself. Which could explain why many marriages between bisexual men and highly sexed women are considerably more successful than the *Till Death Us Do Part* kind. They achieve a balance of love, respect, affection and liberty. But such associations are not for beginners, or everyone. Michelle was able to handle it. 'My own life as a woman has been so rich, and I met this man who made me laugh so much, and anyone who makes me laugh is always halfway into my knickers, but I didn't guess that he was gay. It was a hot day and we were lying on the bed listening to Chopin. It seemed so natural to make love, but he told me I would have to show him what to do. I couldn't believe it, he was not a boy, then he told me and I knew that whatever I said next would be of importance for the rest of his life. I simply said that I didn't care what he was, I loved him as a person, and his joy at this happening to him and his lack of male games made our affair one of the loveliest, most delightful times of my life. I was his first woman, and when I met him in Paris two years later I felt sad to hear that he had gone back to being gay.'

Having the grace to move on, a life of one's own, with no need to put the grappling irons into another's life, is very much a part of becoming a grown woman.

To the young 'pulling' a bloke is part of the power trip, she is happy to have flashed her new outfit or hairdo and left the poor chap standing there with bulging trousers, the older woman is not such a fool; if it's on offer and she has been chatting it up, she might as well get the benefit. Flirting is fun, so is fucking, and the women who have the confidence for a series of lightweight affairs usually have about as much conscience as an erect penis.

No harm done. She blooms, she knows she can get what she wants when she wants it, she cannot be accused of being a prick teaser and he has had an adventure. She can play her new game of confidence like a roulette wheel.

Until it palls.

The young male ego is usually sufficiently resilient to accept the end of an affair; telephone calls left unreturned, pressing dinner dates and unexpected business out of town, and he soon gets the message (except for those clumsy mistakes that end up in the courts and the newspapers). But what if it is the woman who has lowered the drawbridge of her emotions along with her drawers? What if she suddenly becomes mad about the boy? Very dangerous ground. To be captivating is one thing. To become captive of love again with someone who has had the carelessness to be born unsuitably fifteen years too late? It happens. Not often, luckily, but it does. One of the little buggers begins to become more important than all the rest put together, and it's the one who never phones on time, is always late and never has any money. And, as Noel Coward says in his sad little poem, 'I am no good at love' . . . 'I feel the misery of the end the moment it begins. . . .'

I'm afraid this is lecture time. Any woman above the age of forty is too old for unrequited love, or even lust. This is the moment when you must call on all your grown-up friends to come to the aid of the distressed party – only for pride's sake don't tell them the truth, the suggestion that you have been missing them will do. The choice is between amputation and the withered bough. Whoever said 'parting is such sweet sorrow' must have had somebody else hiding in the next doorway. It is not. It is painful and demolishing.

I remember being told for several months, while I hung on to an ailing love affair, that I was old and fat and ugly. It didn't help that he went off with a woman ten years older than myself . . . but what did was that I was put off potatoes and bread for life, lost weight, and found a sweet new young lover.

Michelle, of the great heart, had a similar experience with a Spaniard who was ashamed to introduce her to his friends let alone his parents. 'The difference in our age is too great,' he announced grandly after one year. 'Of course, it was logical,' concedes Michelle, 'he was twenty-three and I was thirty-nine, but I wish I had told him first.'

Getting in there first is Martha Hill's advice, too. 'Have the common sense to move out of an affair as soon as it is more trouble than fun, never let a man get under your skin and destroy you, there is nothing more pathetic than allowing oneself to be rejected.'

Sound advice is not always easy to follow. I recommend a couple of large Scotches with a Sibelius symphony on the record player, a good, wallowing blub, and off to bed exhausted by emotions. You'll feel a lot better in the morning. You won't look it – which is another reason to get it out of the system in one orgy of self-indulgence. Then off to pastures new. The absence of one young man leaves the heart free to get fond of another.

Long-term affairs where the heart has been deeply engaged must leave a scar when they finish. Sadly, the day of reckoning must come when the young man needs to move on; perhaps to have children, to further his career, or simply to take the gift of maturity with which the older woman has endowed him and use it in his own life.

Twenty years later Louise can still recall the pain of parting from her son's tutor. 'Our affair had lasted seven years, it was agony when it broke up, that boy was everything to me. I gave him all my love, the very best of me, and something in the deep of me has never recovered. But

I had given him the confidence, the will to succeed, and he had to go on. That is life.'

But Louise survived, as she knew she would. Her young lover is now a middle-aged and successful man, married with two children, and a life-long friend. She still firmly believes that it would have been wrong to marry him as he so ardently desired. A woman who is attractive to young men in the first place remains so, age does not weary her nor the years destroy, so there have been other involvements, all with men many years younger than herself, and each has given her pleasure, has added to her life. 'It is better to take the risk. Even three or four years are better than nothing. To tell you the truth I *like* to be involved, it is nice to have somebody in your life, I miss the companionship if I am alone, but one must realise that people are what they are and only give what they can.'

Sometimes the ending is a relief as Mala found when she finished an affair with a religious freak. 'I have had some nasty knocks. Sometimes I have discovered the loved one has only been after my money, then you really do fall from a great height – but he was the worst. He spent three months at my house telling me what an arsehole I was. I think I was going through my Zen period and really let him rule my life. All "dramas" had to be avoided, that included all normal, daily routines like organising food, paying bills. And lust. That was a "drama" that had to be conquered. I must have been mad, he put ten years on me, the little fucker, which just proves that not all affairs rejuvenate.

'You can get hurt, I remember crying for three days at the end of one affair, then I looked into the mirror and saw this ravaged sight and decided there and then that I was too old for self-pity. Those three days taught me to be totally realistic about young lovers, that you can't hang on to them because eventually they have to get on with their own lives.'

Most of the women I talked to were philosophical about the risks they were taking. They knew they would survive because their very refusal to become old brought them into constant contact with other generations. All their friends were younger, they had learned that their beauty came from their personality and from what they have to offer, and they were sexually sure of themselves. In the darkness of their wicked, life-loving souls they knew that there were many more young men out there whom they could charm, beguile and entertain until they finally tired of love or sex . . . a day they joyfully could not envisage.

All of them agreed, with smiles broad and bold, that the game was well worth the candle; from seventy to thirty-five, whatever their current circumstance, married, living alone or still playing the field, Martha Hill summed it up for them all. 'Even a year of ecstasy is not to be missed.'

4

OTHER PEOPLES ATTITUDES

Friends, families, foes; only a hermit can travel through life without them. Their unsolicited opinions float round each human being like confetti, assuring that everyone is a source of gossip at least once in their life, even if it's only when they are dead. How much more pleasurable to be the focal point when one is alive. Or is it?

A woman can spend a fortune on her face, figure and clothes. She can lie like a trooper, or evade like a spy the announcement of the number of years she has been on earth. I have myself tried to teach my recalcitrant children that it is not necessary to tell the truth about their ages . . . not, you will understand for *my* benefit, but with the promise that the girls at least will one day be grateful. But the fact is; few of us can deceive by more than a modest number of years. *La différence* between the older woman and her young man is a lot more obvious than she would care to own up to, and the gossips have a field day.

Sometimes the malice is unintentional, sometimes not. There are times when a woman has to hang on to her sense of humour like a deep sea diver to a life-line. My own New Year started off with a pleasant greeting from my host. 'Hello, Sandy darling, is this one of your sons or one of your lovers?' With friends like that who needs foes?

The British have always laughed off their embarrassments, a joke is the obituary of a feeling they say and somewhere along the line one suspects there is a deep-rooted antagonism to the idea of mothers actually enjoying sex. It's not quite proper. It is here that one is fighting deep-seated, unthinking prejudice; the traditional attitudes that are unprepared to take into account just how much women's lives have changed in the last half century. Mothers as people is still a new idea. Mothers as women, that is as sex objects, is even harder to digest.

Most people instinctively resist change. Even a new hairstyle is frequently met with, 'I liked it better the way you had it before' – and most couples feel more distress for *themselves* than for the two people involved in a divorce. A familiar landmark in their lives is being demolished and *they* will have to re-think a friendship.

So when a woman takes to younger men she is disturbing a whole set of comfortably held opinions. Like: a woman needs a man to pay the bills; only young women are sexually attractive; there has got to be something wrong with a man who fancies a woman nearly old enough to be his mother. Were she to arrive at a social gathering with an ageing millionaire-widower on her arm she would be congratulated on her good fortune at finding a suitable partner to provide for her imminent old age. The fact that his skin looked like crêpe lavatory paper would be considered irrelevant. Arriving, radiant, with a handsome young man who obviously adores her makes waves that might ripple all the way out to her friends' sequestered shores.

Shirley Young found out for herself when she announced that she was marrying Barry. 'To be honest most of my friends and employers thought I was totally mad. I

had been married, was financially secure, pretty good looking in those days [she still is] and sharply dressed. They
thought I would more than match my prowess, sophistication and glamour. And here was this chap, a fabric salesman on £3000 a year when I was earning nearly that a
month! They said, "he's very nice and sweet and keep him
as a lover but you should be marrying someone like the
chairman of Shell or Rank Xerox."

'They genuinely thought I was capable of it and they
were disappointed in me; they thought I had let them
down and chosen beneath them, not me. It was their pres-
tige that was destroyed, not mine, I was very happy with
my fella. Now he has come up to their expectations and is
extremely successful, but it was tough at first.'

Britt Ekland is the latest one to come under fire. A newspaper article commenting on her two failed marriages and
the much publicised break-up with Rod Stewart, makes
much of her announcement that she has now turned her
sights on younger men 'because she wants no permanent
commitment'. Is it vanity or the desire to prove to herself
and everyone else that she is still attractive, the paper asks,
nastily adding that at the age of thirty-seven she now has
this preoccupation with adolescents. Just what you need
when you are trying to put your life together.

I've been there at the receiving end of gratuitous comments from colleagues, acquaintances and fast-becoming-
ex friends. 'Well, if you will run around with boys . . .'
chauvinistically ignoring that they are chasing girls little
older than their own daughters. It is useless to fume, the
commentators are blind to comparisons.

Nobody actually considers that a woman might actually prefer the company of the young, virile escort who
makes her laugh and then takes her home to screw her all

night . . . oh, no, it has got to be some inherent weakness in her character. She obviously feels inadequate as a woman which is why she doesn't fancy the men of her own age. . . . It's so funny you would have to cry if you didn't laugh!

It is an attitude that will change with time and familiarity as the numbers of open liaisons between older women and younger men increase. Until then, the situation is bound to meet with resentment and unrealised fury, that essence of all bigotry. And until then it will have to be dealt with by the protagonists, the grown women and the younger men, with the happy knowledge that they at least are minding their own business and living the life they want.

Friends often assume a posture of protectiveness and from that stance feel privileged to deliver some extremely unkind cuts. 'Come out of your cloud,' they told Niké, 'he must have a mother complex.' Unfortunately in her case the friends were right, as she discovered later when her boy-friend's mother came thundering into town, demanding of her son, 'What are you doing with this *old* woman?' And Niké was all of thirty-five!

Real friends disguise their true feelings exquisitely, if not from you at least from themselves. Women, seeing you seated beside an enraptured young man, will make an enormous effort to cross a crowded room to enquire tenderly about your children, they will ensure the hapless fella that you are indeed a wonderful mother, then ask, ever so casually, how old they are now? Watching his eyes do a swift calculation and the radiant glow of anticipation fade from your face will be more than sufficient compensation for their efforts.

This is the moment to come out of the corner fighting,

87

lady. Remember that if they are big enough they are old enough. But fight clean; never, ever be tempted to such vulgarities as, 'Dear Maggie, she is one of my *oldest* friends.' Of course all is fair in lust and war – and a silly self-denigrating remark about the mistakes you made as a child-bride can soon restore a young man's computer-balanced enthusiasm. Just don't get carried away on a sea of lies; innuendos, yes, ignored truths, yes, but outright lies can form a terrible trap. I once ended up so miscalculating that I realised the following day that I should have been in the *Guinness Book of Records* for giving birth at the age of six.

Another neat trick women can pull is to sail up to you and your current pretty number with this one : 'Darling, who was that absolutely gorgeous young man I saw you with at so-and-so's party? . . . I fancied him no end.'

Now what to do?

Well you can't pretend you don't remember who she is talking about without the risk of appearing as a cross between Superwoman and a walking female Dracula consuming young men for breakfast . . . without even the courtesy of remembering the poor little bugger's names. You can't state that he was an absolute disaster for fear of frightening the newest recruit away. And you can't very well give the impression that it must have been your son or your brother. This woman is your *friend*, remember?

It has to be table-turning time. Of course you recall him, and he fancied her too, had even rung to find out her telephone number. Surely he had rung by now? No? Oh dear, what a shame. And then it is time to turn your full attention back to your companion. It's amazing how attractive a woman can look when her eyes are glittering with triumphant malice! It is at such moments that a

88

woman must concentrate on her self-confidence, lean heavily on her sense of humour and promise herself to never, ever give a woman friend an even break.

I must admit that the most wickedly funny incident that ever happened to me was when I was out one Saturday evening with Jill Evans, a bright Welsh witch from the *Daily Mirror*. We were bemoaning the dearth of talent in our love lives when we noticed a reasonably good-looking bloke trying to engage our attention. He got it. From both of us. Full blaze of charm. Then nature called and I disappeared to the loo. On my return Jill was looking very sparkly, and while he was ordering drinks she leaned across to me. 'He thinks you're very attractive and wanted to know all about you. I told him you were my best friend . . . and wasn't it a shame about the fits?'

About the what?

'About the fits. I told him you were very intelligent but you had this affliction, but that he wasn't to worry because they only started when you laughed.' The rotten little cow's face was gleaming . . . and I, of course, was laughing myself silly. Poor man, he made his drink last as long as he decently could then left. But not before we had both got our come-uppance; the long-haired, navy-blue sweatered companion we had both taken for granted as his son turned out to be his girl-friend.

Jill and I have had a declared pax ever since.

But if you think your woman friends are provocative and sly . . . just wait till you start introducing your young man to the men who have known you ten to fifteen years. Particularly if they have always hoped to get into your knickers one day.

The male ego is ever a fragile thing; and men in their forties are well aware of opportunities missed without you

89

presenting them with unsolicited evidence. Offended and nervous at having to deal with someone whose status as your lover proclaims that he must be fit and sexy, they quickly retreat into spite. Affable spite, of course, as they carefully manoeuvre the conversation through a string of incidents, dates and names as long as a kite tail. Your past. Just in case you had neglected to reveal your age. Should it not be just their nose that is put out of joint, so to speak, they get worse, as Jane found out.

She had been conducting an affair with a middle-aged film producer, organising her life round his, when she met Hans who seduced her over dinner and three bottles of champagne. It had to be the one night the producer rang at three in the morning. And at four. And five. And at her office to find out where she had been all night. She had to own up and tell him she had found someone new.

Months later they all met at a party. '*This* is not what you gave *me* up for?' was the enraged reaction, and the room was filled with the blossom of hate.

Looks like hell will have to find space for men scorned too.

Acquaintances are quick to add their twopenn'orth. 'I see you are out with your mother again,' is proffered with a smile that makes your feet ache to reach for the speaker's well-displayed teeth. But taking umbrage is strictly against the rules, as is encouraging a lover to punch the offender in the mouth; indifference or wit are the two best defences.

One gratuitous comment my lover received at the beginning of our relationship was aimed at discomforting both of us. 'Don't you think she is a bit old for you?' ran the pleasantry when I was out of earshot.

'Why don't you go and ask *her* that?' was the sensible reply.

The man gulped his drink and fled. There are some advantages to having a reputation for a sharp tongue.

But there are times when you can't win. When my lover moved in there was much nudging and winking that he had parked his shoes under my bed because I had some money and his business had recently failed. A couple of months later and I was standing in the pub alone, which was all the more noticeable as we had been inseparable. Where was he, they wanted to know. Out at work, was the reply. 'Why, you mean old cow, fancy sending him out to work with all *your* money !' was their scandalised reaction.

I think its called 'heads you win; tails I lose'.

Molly Parkin and Patrick reckoned they have probably each lost half of their former friends, which is about average for any marriage. Most of the women I interviewed say that their affairs with younger men have injured some of their friendships permanently but all admitted their need to hang on to others – either to return to at wound-licking time, or for a good laugh; a shared past is too precious to throw away. Joan Bakewell says that Jack sometimes gets sulky about her 'Cambridge-mafia' but most of her friends are very relieved that they no longer have a neurotic woman on their hands. Erica says that Graham sometimes makes bitchy remarks about 'your friends'. 'It's just that it must be extremely boring for him to hear them chatting about what happened in 1949.' But Lynda feels that you have to learn to mix life-styles, to get on with his friends too, and finds that her friends' love of her enhances her image in her boyfriend's eyes.

Louise and Michael walked into a suave hotel in Nice, across the foyer a friend of hers, a contemporary, screamed, 'Ah, I see you have another one of those gigolos with you!' Grown-up lady that she is, Louise still wanted to die on the spot. Yet when Michael took her to meet his family in Texas she was treated like a queen, getting on famously with his mother who was a few years younger than herself.

Meeting the mother of the young man in a serious affair is bound to give cause for trepidation, particularly if Mum has led a sheltered family life. Not many people can have made such an inauspicious beginning as Shirley Young, whom I have mentioned before. At the time she was thirty, ambitious, divorced, with a son of four from her first marriage, an establishment in Cavendish Street and a housekeeper to run it. Barry was a youth of twenty-five just starting his career as a fabric salesman and sharing a flat with two friends. They had been lovers for a year when he decided it was time for Shirley to meet his parents. The weekend was arranged but at the last moment Barry had a business meeting and Shirley set off alone.

'I said, "Are you sure you told them and that I am expected?" and he said, "Yes." I arrived after three hours driving through thunder and rain with a small child and two huge labrador dogs in a small second-hand Mini estate all the way from London to the Fenlands in Norfolk, late at night.

'I knocked on the door and his mother answered it. I said, "I'm Shirley." '

'She said "Who?" '

'He hadn't told her a thing about me!'

Personally I think I would have driven all the way back and broken a bottle over his head, but when his stunned mother had recovered from the shock she accepted her worldly future daughter-in-law with open arms and they have been friends ever since.

92

Erica has been in the privileged position of piggy-in-the-middle with sons, lovers and mothers. 'I am bang in the middle between Graham and his mother, ten years exactly either way, what amazes me is that his parents absolutely love my children, they are charming to me and never make me feel ninety-five, so when my son introduced me to his girl-friend who was sixteen or so years older than him it was easy for me. I liked her, she was a mad, giggly creature who looked about twenty-two and I much preferred her to any of his younger girl-friends.'

Gillian Bobroff was less fortunate with her previous mothers-in-law. She says unforgivingly, 'My child was taken away when he was eleven months old and I only met up with him again when he was sixteen. The other mother-in-law was orthodox Jewish and deliberately broke up the marriages of both her son and daughter, each of whom had married outside the faith.'

Stories like that just go to show how lucky actress Louise Fletcher is with her lover's mother. Pamela Mason, ex-wife of actor James, when asked to comment on the thriving love affair between Ms Fletcher and her twenty-two-year-old son said, 'I think it is great, so what if it is a disaster in fifteen years' time?'

With the average marriage between contemporaries lasting about eight years, she is right, there are no guarantees in love or life.

In fact a woman is more likely to have at least a certain amount of trouble balancing out her own life-style and sexual, loving needs with that of her growing children.

The old Stag at Bay syndrome has many aspects. Daughters in their late teens can be very competitive; they can envy their mother's style, financial and emotional freedom just as much as she envies their fine, taut skin, firm breasts and youthful agility. The competition can be mental, too. A woman cooking Sunday breakfast for her lusted one and teenage family, listening to them all discussing the lyrics of pop songs, South American politics and the virtues of one pox hospital over another doesn't feel all that great. Except in bloody age that is. My daughters and I, being a supportive family, formed an alliance for going to parties together. The rule was; anything under thirty was theirs, anything over thirty was mine.

It didn't work. I had just reached the age where the young men fancied me, a situation I was unused to and couldn't believe in (then), and the older men who were fascinated by my nubile daughters were whisked off, sensibly, by their wives. Invariably we found ourselves going home together. Three very disappointed ladies.

We had another rule. That any bloke who ensnared one of us did *not* get another bite at the Fawkes family. Once they had donated their golden apple, so to speak, that was their lot, no flitting, they had laid their bedmate and must keep to it.

That didn't work either. A mixture of their cunning and our carelessness in exchanging information and we found several fellas were able to boast about two down and one to go!

But the alliance stood. We are, and I expect always will be, friends, accepting the changes in our personalities at each new stage in our lives. There is much to be gained for the children of a happy, fulfilled, if unconventional mother. The knowledge that she is moving into a positive phase of her own life enables them to develop an independence, both sexually and mentally, free of guilt. A woman who is busy with her career and love-life can communicate

94

with her children on a grown-up, equal level, sharing with them the turmoils and delights of living in a changeable world. She can give them confidence, an assurance that the bad times can be met and dealt with. She is still warm with life.

It is the clinging, pathetic parent whose children visit her out of duty and with dread who is most likely to be subconsciously punishing her children for her own disappointments, her own halted development. Resentment of the younger generation's chance is rich fertilising ground for bitterness and lethargy.

A young lover can be a bridge between the two generations, partly because his interests will be half-way between them (his attitudes and education will be post-war, like her children's, even though he is ahead of them) and partly because his presence informs them that their mother is a person in her own right. She is neither their property nor some nebulous Earth Mother figure to be taken for granted. Her sexuality clears the air.

Most of the sons and daughters of the women I interviewed were extremely good friends with their mothers, seeking her company of their own volition. As one of them said, 'She is where the action is, she is attractive to such a variety of people we always have fun.' Another, a son, said, 'Because she is happy there is room for love between us, she's not demanding like some of my friends' mothers – mind you, I'm more likely to get a home-cooked meal at their place ! But there isn't this generation gap, I get along with her friends and she with mine. We can both explore each other's places.'

Girls, once they have overcome the very natural rivalry and sense of threat that an attractive, lively mother presents, are quick to admit to the long-term advantage.

'It can be difficult at first,' said the daughter of one volatile and sexy mum, 'you get fed-up with being introduced just as someone's daughter, you want to be recognised as yourself, but my mother has given me one great gift . . . and that is not to *fear* age. She has taken a lot of knocks both in her private life and in her work but I have watched *her* develop over the years and I now know that I have time to do the same. I don't have to panic.' Yet another young woman was able to say of her mother, 'What is funny is the way she worries about her age. She is having a marvellous time, *I'm* the one that has the struggle ahead! But she does give me a sense of security in that I can see there is plenty of life to be had as well as marriage and children. And she still believes in love, which is comforting in this day and age.'

It is a tougher road for sons initially. In adolescence they can feel embarrassed and ashamed when their mother appears at functions looking years younger than their friends' parents. Martha Hill's son remembers walking ahead of his mother when she visited him at school wearing a black and white leather outfit, that is until one of his friends *and* one of the masters asked him who his gorgeous visitor was.

Later they can become downright belligerent. Adolescent boys being brought up by their female parent have enough problems without seeing their mother being treated as a sex object, being cuddled, caressed and propositioned at an age when they are sorting out their own masculinity. They need a father figure but have not the habit of accepting authority from a man, and to expect a young lover to take over the role of boss is to invite disaster. He has neither the inclination nor the training. The sublimated rage of a son taking refuge in rejection, scruffiness and a generally negative attitude towards everything in opposition to an ardent young lover's sense of achievement can lead to rows and even violence.

On an 'antlers-locked' level this is not entirely unhealthy, a boy can take out on a lover emotions that would be denied him were his father still the challenger to his mother's affections.

One young man whose mother had a lover near his age admits, 'We used to have terrible punch-ups, but now I look back we probably would have done anyhow, we were at the age to enjoy it. I suppose I was jealous but I can laugh at it now, he is still with her, she is happy and when we all meet we get along all right.'

'I still feel he's a cunt,' said another son cheerfully, 'but I accept him as part of her life and he's very good for a touch when I'm skint.' But one lad, aged twenty, whose mother's lover is thirty, said, 'Yeah, well, it is all a bit embarrassing. I know he loves her, but when we are all out together and I meet some of my mates he never knows quite which way to turn. My mates would never take the piss out of my mum but they think he is fair game, so he's got to show that he is older than us because he is with her but he wants to be one of the lads as well. I mean, they like him but we usually drift off after a while, it's easier.'

There can be no doubt that for a while it is harder for a son to accept a sexually successful, vibrant, working mum, particularly in this age of unemployment. Even their girlfriends are likely to look unformed beside her, another knock at their manhood, but eventually your lover and sons can become friends. That's when you could find yourself sitting in front of the television watching *Match of the Day*, boxing, golfing championships and athletics.

Whoever invented the Primrose Path forgot to mention that it is surrounded by brambles and gin traps.

Accepting that the bond between offspring and a rebellious mother will usually be solved (even David Niven finally learned to love the mum whose lover had sent him to Dickensian schools) children must not be expected to make room in their lives for the man in hers. Listening to men who grew up in more conventional circumstances you will find that they are more or less equally divided between those who loved their stepfathers and those who could not.

One's childrens' feelings must be respected because they are genuine and based on complex emotions that have nothing to do with their mother's physical desires. The man who fascinates her may not interest them at all. Some are loving enough to be polite, the painful time for a woman deeply involved with a younger man is when her children feel strongly enough to issue ultimatums.

Sometimes, a woman is forced to make a choice between her children and her lover, a horrible situation for which there are no guide-lines. This is more frequent when the age gap between the couple is great enough for the children to be older than the lover. One woman who married a boy of nineteen when her son was already twenty-two has not seen her son for many years, even though he is now a happily married man. 'He has told me that I will not see or hear from him again until I get rid of Peter – Christmas and birthdays go by without even a card. But I can't help it – it's my life and I love Peter. I just have to hope that one day my son will be generous enough to change his attitude.'

Other women get round this almost biological discomfort between lover and kin by meeting their children alone, a conflict of loyalties that needs to be worked out very honestly. There could be a basis of unresolved jealousy to be overcome; one's mother feeling love, and a sexual love at that, with a person younger than oneself cannot be an easy emotion to deal with. It certainly adds to the vague burden of guilt, however unnecessary, that accompanies the unconventional coupling. As ever, there are no rules, and Louise's grandchild happily calls Michael '*grandpère*', and at thirty-three Michael is proud of his title.

Friends, families . . . and now the foe.

Alas, the woman who makes a play for younger men is also fencing with the eternal foe: time. Not the time ahead with its threat of wrinkles and grey hair – but the time running backwards in the form of much, much younger women.

Girls, in fact.

Girls, as we all remember, have little or no conscience when it comes to giving their charms a gallop, and a man who lives with a woman ten years his senior has double attractiveness for the girl ten years his junior. For one thing he must be fully experienced to keep his lady happy (and a girl's longing for masterful tuition endures long after the loss of her hymen) – and of course he must really be *dying* for someone young.

Devoted as he may be, no man is immune to flattery and the girls will try playing games with your fella. They will flaunt their youth, their only true possession, and sometimes they will succeed. They will use ruthless stratagems like, 'I wish you were *my* mother, mine is so stuffy,' . . . 'It must have been awful before they had television – what did you all do?'

Half-innocent these remarks may well be. I remember

doing a classic myself many years ago. A nervous, pregnant bride, I was asked to a smart party where I overheard
two famous women journalists saying that they had always
intended to have another child when they were forty. To
my eternal shame I asked, 'And did you?' It was only
afterwards I discovered they were in their mid-thirties.
Girls of today are more knowing, they have been taught
the value of a healthy sex life and they, too, are avaricious
for experience. They are only half aware of the threat that
their bright, eager bodies and faces can represent. Their
attempts at luring another woman's lover away may be
crude, even laughable at times, and can mostly be ignored,
but of course a percentage of the young men will feel the
need to return to their own age group and will do so.
Jealousy is a waste of energy, possessiveness is a negation
of one's own hard-fought-for freedom and if a man really
feels the need to change to a younger partner then one
must let him go.

It is here that the most important attitude of all comes
in; the attitude to self, and the survival of that self. Nobody's yesterdays return; not for the girls, the young men,
nor the older women. Today is all important, and the daily
maintenance of a fulfilled, sexually active, grown woman
must be fertilised by a sense of self-respect. She has come
this far, she has made the best of her life and now has
something very worthwhile to offer. Not just her sexuality,
not just her personality, but her experience as a female
makes her a valuable person. Remembering this she should
be able to deal with the occasional loss, to recognise that
there are still many amusements and opportunities left in
the world . . . and move on with grace.

5

TILTING AT THE WORLD
CAN IT WORK?

Perhaps the most punishing moment in a mature woman's life comes the morning after the night before. The young man is ready to leave. 'See you,' he says cheerfully, not discourteously but definitely anxious to be on his way. Experienced by now, she never says, 'When?' A chaste and formal kiss on the cheek and he has gone. Forever? Not always. Some of them are more than shits that pass in the night and the phone will ring suggesting a meal, a drink, the theatre. And he will be standing there, on time, and as happy at seeing you as a dog with two pricks in a street full of lamp-posts.

It is very sweet. And doesn't always work out. That second meeting can often prove that the only thing you had in common the time you met was mutual need. But what if it wasn't an error? What if one meeting leads to another, and another and another?

A woman begins to mellow as she learns to trust her man; she can rely on him being at the appointed place, he is not playing vain games at her expense, he is not after her money, a roof over his head, or using her to further his career. This is the moment to temper lust with caution. It is about now he will turn up at a date, albeit apologetically, with a chic carrier bag containing a pair of socks, underpants and a shirt with the excuse that he has an early morning appointment. When he leaves, his discarded clothes have formed a territorial encroachment.

Does she want it? The answer depends on many things. Her career, family life, her maturity (she may not be in the mood for a stable relationship), even her other lovers. Those socks, which she will automatically wash, may turn out to be a bigger trap than a young girl being late with her period.

But if she has stopped thinking of him as a useful escort or stud to keep her juices going and begun to think of him as a lovable human being who gets tired, hungry, farts, gets pissed and is a bit of a darling, she is probably ready to allow him to enter her life as well as her body.

Can it work? The answer is so glaringly silly that one wonders where the prejudice could have come from. It all depends on the two people involved. Just like any other partnership.

Of the women I have talked to who have spent years with a man younger than themselves some have been through the formality of marriage while others haven't thought it necessary. And while willing to mouth allow-ances for the occasional foolish mistake, all of them, the men included, have been strongly into monogamy. Con-trary to expectations it is the men who, having found an all round satisfactory relationship, are the most wary of casting a wandering eye.

Patrick Hughes when he married Molly Parkin was adamant. 'We made certain rules, and we have kept to them. We have never spent a night apart. We never do . . .'

'Not even if it injures our careers,' a very chuffed Molly pops in.

'Because I wouldn't trust her and she wouldn't trust me for one moment, it's as simple as that. There is no trust in our relationship whatsoever.'

'He was a terrible womaniser,' states Molly piously. 'Really it is self-awareness. We know that we are both attractive, we know we both drink and we know that you can get to a certain point of an evening . . . you've had this dinner, a professional dinner . . . and then something catches your eye. Well, it's if it moves, fuck it, isn't it?'

Yes, Molly, I know what you mean.

Any doubts Molly and Patrick may have entertained about their own standards were dispersed when a grand friend of theirs went off to cover the Edinburgh Festival for an esteemed Sunday newspaper. 'He went away on his own and returned with a new love. He was sixty, the new mistress was seventy and the girl he left behind him was forty, she was destroyed. She couldn't understand that if she had been there it wouldn't have happened.'

It is a fact that being in love does not strike one blind. My own well-trained eye sometimes spots what would have been a nice piece of bed fodder but I agree with Martha Hill when she declares, 'This is my body and I can do with it what I like . . . but, once I'm in love, then it is given utterly and completely.'

A woman's greater age and experience can be an asset when the relationship is threatened though one has to bear in mind that all these philosophical statements are made from comfortably secure alliances. As Molly puts it, 'I am frightened of losing him really, I was never frightened of losing people of my own age, but I also know now that if it were to end it wouldn't annihilate me at all, I know I would just go on and find somebody else.'

Erica has the same feelings. 'There is always a risk,

especially as your younger man heads towards forty, the classic restless period. I don't dare think about it but I don't live in fear as I did with my husband. Perhaps I have more confidence now, because although the thought is intolerable, I know that if we did break up I should be able to cope.'

Shirley, too, has speculated on how she would react if Barry started fancying young birds. 'Well, in my first marriage I was anything but faithful so I know it can happen, but I think it depends on the state of the marriage at the time. If he had an affair I think I would sit down and say, "You have obviously had an affair because our relationship is not good, what can we do about it?" But if our marriage was good and he was away on a trip and he fancied some raving beauty of eighteen I would be hurt, but I'd pluck my tongue out before I said anything rotten. Once I was assured of what it was, and we have built our marriage in total honesty, that it was a one night stand and he had done it because he fancied her like mad I would say, "O.K. baby, please don't let it happen again, but if it does please don't let me hear about it from someone else." I would be genuinely hurt but I would do my utmost not to be destructive.

'In fact he told me when it very nearly did happen. He was away for three weeks in the USA and one of the models was an unbelievably beautiful seventeen-year-old, and, as it happened, he lost her to a pop star, that was my good fortune, not his. But if it had happened he says he would have told me. So what am I supposed to do? Divorce my lovely husband because he was away three weeks and fancied this bird? Not bloody likely.' Lest she sounds too noble to stomach she adds with a wicked grin, 'I know what I'd be like in those circumstances . . . three weeks in five-star surroundings, all paid for, relaxed and a handsome young man? Believe me, I'd have to fight the devil to keep my hands off him. Judge others as you would yourself, baby.'

I think the saddest conversation I listened to was with a man in just that situation. He had been married for eleven years to a woman twelve years older than himself and was unable to bear the thought of his wife becoming fifty this year. 'She was thirty-nine when I met her and I was twenty-seven but it didn't seem to matter then. She had three children by her first marriage and we have one of our own, she has been a marvellous wife and mother and a terrific support in my career. [He is a painter.] I feel so guilty, but I can't face the thought of making love to a woman of fifty, it's illogical I know. Somehow I feel desperate, as if now is my last chance at youth, young girls.' Life, with one of its ironic tricks, has thrown him right into the path of temptation with a job at a leading art school and as a bitter compliment to the honesty of their relationship, his wife knows how he feels. 'I feel terribly sorry for him,' she says, without a trace of self-pity. 'I can only hope it will pass. Soon.'

I feel I should own up here. I still sulk, rant and rave if I sense that some bird is after my fella, and it isn't really young ones that cause me concern but the attractive personalities in my own age group. After all, if a young man fancies one older woman he might well move on to another. It isn't ladylike to make scenes in public and keeping your cool is important but that doesn't mean to say you can't slag him off when you get him home, the only thing is that when you tell him to fuck off he might do just that.

But most true relationships survive the odd, alcoholic row. Mine does for the simple reason that whatever we have screamed at each other the night before, even if on waking his brain says, 'She's a rotten, possessive, jealous old cow,' his cock says, 'You please yourself, I want it.' Thank heavens for stamina.

Shirley and Barry had to face a bit of harsh reality earlier this year when she was rushed to hospital for a hysterectomy. 'It isn't age that is my hang-up but the fact that although I have a son by my first marriage and have fulfilled myself as a woman, the one thing Barry would have liked in our marriage is a child. Before the operation there was always a faint chance that I might become pregnant again, the doctors said it was very unlikely but it was something for him to hold on to, now he has to know there isn't any chance at all. What worries me is that by loving him I am stopping him having the one thing he desires most of all. When I tell him that, he just says, "Nonsense, you are my life and I have my beautiful stepson and everything's all right." But he is a little vain, all men are, and his great joy would have been a little furry-headed Barry running around the house and garden.

'Sometimes I even think I should get out, set him free to get what he wants, then I think, why should I, it's not like me to give up. If it is that much of a force it must be his decision. Instead I hope by being affectionate, a good, loving wife and a great friend, and by making his life as comfortable as posible I may make up for it.'

From the way Barry was marking off the days to when they could get at it again after her operation Shirley need have no worries!

But Barry and Shirley have been together for twelve years, they faced their problem as an established couple. For others, where the woman is fast approaching forty or even past it, and the man is ten or more years her junior, the fact of whether or not he wants children, or will want them in the future, must come up for discussion before the relationship can be allowed to develop too deeply.

Contraception plus the availability of legal abortion has freed most men from the shot-gun wedding and many men now reach their thirties without having given a thought to fatherhood. They have been free to travel the world, to enjoy a variety of sexual alliances, and the sort of independence their fathers probably envy. A barrier has been lifted; the proof of their masculinity no longer lies in the pudding club. But will the young man think differently when he has settled down with his new and older partner? She will probably have children of her own, near grown up at that. He will be entering a life which is both adventurous and stable – and loving. But will he, in a few years time, bump into an old school chum, and listen with a pang of envy to the pride and love in his friend's voice as he talks about his offspring? And will that pang grow into a gnawing need to know that special kind of love himself?

It is a subject that has to be thoroughly aired once mutual love has been offered and accepted. A young man, finding a satisfactory and worthwhile love, really means 'forever' when he says it; a mature woman has usually learned that 'forever' can indeed seem like a lifetime towards the end of a marriage or an affair ... but that in measurable time it may be ten years at the most. Of course she hopes that this time it will work but she has seen the men in her life change, grow. The responsibility for delaying a man's biological need for parenthood is not to be taken lightly. On the encouraging side Glenn Wilson states that there is no conclusive evidence that *either* sex has a drive to have children, an attitude endorsed by many young career women of today. 'I think,' he says, 'both genders have a drive to look after children and a drive to have sex but I don't think there is any drive that links the two.'

The couples I talked to where the woman was at an age where child-bearing could be dangerous had all considered this aspect of their joined futures. Patrick has had a vasectomy to save Molly the painful periods she suffered with her coil, but he already has three sons by his first marriage.

Jack Emery came to the decision that being husband to Joan and stepfather to her two children was a sufficient gift from life. 'I thought about it a lot, particularly when my mother died and I began to feel "what am I going to leave behind?" ... but I came to the conclusion that I didn't feel any real need to have children. I suppose in that way I shall never again be part of a family in the sense of gut relationship but it doesn't make me feel inadequate.

'Marriage was the strong gesture for both of us – we married in church with a service that had visual and verbal beauty – and it's going to last. Joan is a woman whom living up to is a pleasure, her mind is as curious as any youngster's and her body is just as beautiful.'

For Michael the question was academic; Louise was comfortably past her menopause and he was in his mid-twenties. 'It's funny, even as a kid I was bored with my own age group. I played bridge a lot to get away from them, and all the girls went off to college to find a husband. I didn't want to get married and have children, so that's how I really got started with older women. I never have wanted children. I was brought up in an unhappy family relationship and I saw a lot of unhappiness amongst married couples around me, and I thought ... why get involved in all that, bringing children into the world when you don't know if you are going to love them or they are going to love you? I cleaned my slate of all that. Louise and I have so much in common, we both like travel, enjoy eating and drinking, and she has so much energy the age thing doesn't have anything to do with it, really.'

The sharing of life rather than the reproducing of it appears to be a very positive trend amongst couples where the woman's career is flourishing. As a woman begins to ease her way out of her thirties it does seem that the sound of a hi-fi is preferable to the patter of tiny feet.

Lynda Trapnell is an entertainers' business manager, successful enough to have her own mortgage and old enough to have a marriage, a live-in relationship and a string of handsome young lovers behind her. She is thirty-nine and fast approaching the last days of the age of decision; to have or not to have a child, a question made all the more poignant by the fact that she is in love with a man of thirty-one.

'It has to be such a *conscious* decision now, you have to go to the doctor and ask him to remove the coil and he is duty bound to ask you to think very carefully. Frank and I once talked about it and he doesn't want them any more than I do but at the same time he is not keen on the idea of adoption if we wait a few years. I have to admit that I look to the future with blinkers, I don't want to be a lonely old lady but having a child is no guarantee against that, neither is marriage. Of course one half of me would love to rush off to the registry office, probably the same half that talks about having a child, but a relationship needs a lot of work before you can put that half of you first.

'But if I decided to go ahead and later he changed his mind, I would let him go. I would suffer anger and misery, but I would own up to never having played safety, that I'd lost.'

The medical hazards of giving birth in later years are well documented, but the risks to the romantic love affair between the older woman and the younger man are perhaps not so well known. Chillingly it was the women who *had* taken the step that Lynda was discussing that were having severe marital troubles; those shining young men, doting fathers that they may be, often suffer a deep and destructive restlessness when they find themselves *tied* to an older woman. There are tenuous times in all marriages but it would seem that the chances of breaking down are greater if a woman exchanges her role of star in his firmament for an over-tired, nappy-washing homebody.

Youth, frustration and drink are not a happy combination, and guilt doesn't add much of a gloss either. Violent rows, a screaming child, and a woman ageing at vampirical speed are a long way from the fun and glamour of parties, expense account lunches and an ardent grope in the back of a taxi. That's not tilting at the world – that's the tilt of the pinball machine.

It was comforting to note that in the *good* marriages and long-distance partnerships between younger men and grown-up ladies there was an extraordinarily positive, sustained warmth between them; as if their constant surprise at the accidental bridging of such discrepant birthdates was a new discovery at each meeting. They are tremendously supportive of, and loyal to, each other, probably the result of earlier comments from the outside world; they have closed ranks and do not make derogatory remarks about their partners in public. Also they actually *look* at each other when they are speaking, their familiarity breeds respect not contempt. Being the explorers of a different kind of love they are prepared to nurture each other's egos. As Erica says, 'We like talking to each other too much, the only time we ever have rows is when one of us has had too much to drink.' Like many other aspects of people's lives their appearance is the outward sign of the inner effort each makes. As Joan Bakewell comments, 'I resolved never to put on weight and consciously take a lot more care than if I had a fat and balding husband.' And Molly and Patrick demonstrate their togetherness in their mode of dress, outrageously, elegantly pop, each the perfect foil, a compliment to their relationship.

Perhaps it is an awareness of effort for each other that keeps such electricity going, perhaps it is just that in a world of grey, neurotic, Jules Ffieffer-type relationships, to see two people giving to each other so willingly is a rare sight. Or perhaps it is just their sexuality that sets a room alight?

Actually it was Shirley who told me that I hadn't asked the one question that other people always asked her . . . 'Can an older woman keep up with a young man's sex drive?' Frankly, the question hadn't occurred to me since all the women I had talked to were so obviously enjoying every aspect of their partnership; and they certainly didn't look worn out. All of them mentioned the abundance of their sex lives, the joys of being freed from the missionary position and the pleasures of partnering a sex drive that can keep it up!

From Glenn Wilson I later learned that according to

male folklore there is only one thing more difficult than getting a woman started sexually . . . getting her stopped again.

This endorsed Shirley's comment. 'In this day and age I think many more women set the pace of a sexual relationship, although I also think that a lot of women aren't much use in bed until they are at least twenty-eight, and from then on they get better, not worse. I know I lost my virginity at fourteen though I didn't have an orgasm until I was twenty-four.

'As we get older we lose our inhibitions (sometimes through the naughty scrapes we have got ourselves into) so we offer much more freedom in sex. After all, they do say that sex is all in the mind – so we have had longer to think about it!'

Lots of women seem to have taken several years before they actually learned to come. I know I was very late, and at first I thought that this was probably due to our lack of sex education, something that was corrected by the feminist influence on women's magazines. But even younger women, those who have been on the Pill and known of the Big O since their teens said that their ability to enjoy sex has grown with the years. Most women look back on their twenties as a difficult, emotionally inhibited time. It is the growth of self-knowledge plus the variety of their experience that enables them to be sexually satisfied, which in its turn is complimentary to a young man and certainly one of the reasons he comes back for more, thus allowing a casual sexual liaison to develop into at least a loving friendship.

But, as I have to keep reminding myself, there is more to life than bed and learning to live with someone new and young inevitably brings about changes in a woman.

Gentler; more tolerant; patient; softer as a person, were all descriptions of themselves I heard from the women who had embarked on real alliances with men younger than themselves. This is probably due to the relaxation of anxieties, the late discovery that one's lovability rate does not depend on physical perfection. A grown woman whose life has been living proof of her own defects, who has been lonely and afraid, and yet had the courage to cope, is unlikely to turn her nose up at her man's weaknesses. Her indulgence of mistakes is based on the knowledge of her own ability for error. She is bound to be kinder and more caring because she has learned that recriminations, cruelty and haggling over small stupidities does not work.

Gillian Bobroff says, 'I feel far more understanding as a person, and now willingly do the things *he* wants to do. I used to be brutally selfish and would never do anything to please someone else, and strangely, I enjoy my life more now. I think the mature woman is not only *not* domineering, she is not demanding either.'

It may well be that former experience has taught the women to expect less of others, that careers are as important as relationships, or that the responsibility for happiness lies within themselves, not on the lovely, firm, young shoulders of their lover.

It may also be that the very pattern of their lives together, the freedom to give undivided loyalty to each other, the exquisite selfishness of their life-style, helps to sustain an otherwise unusual love affair. Because when they work these partnerships are remarkably sound and, interestingly, the age difference seems to disappear, the couple become unaware of the gap in their birth-dates and genuinely see each other only as people.

Of course there are constant reminders of that gap; as

Joan Bakewell says, 'The War is the great divider' . . . and I had an unwelcome illustration of this myself later as we sat watching television. On to the screen flashed the headline 'Dresden, 13 February 1945' . . . 'Christ, I was one month and three days old' . . . announced my lover. A wallop round the head with a pillow was all he got for his pains. These are the times when it pays to have a sense of humour and a swift right hook.

So when the relationship is a happy one it would seem that the age difference is of little or no importance. And it is very noticeable in those circumstances that whilst the woman becomes softer, looks younger and obviously enjoys allowing the girl in her to bloom again, the young men are consistently more mature, protective and manly. They become sure of themselves socially and sexually. They have been given the confidence of love and they respond generously with admiration, encouragement and a warm steadfastness that allows both partners to expand as human beings.

It doesn't sound much like a mother/son relationship, does it?

6

METAMORPHOSIS

Chamber's Twentieth Century Dictionary defines the word 'menopause' as the ending of menstruation, the change of life. It comes from the Greek, *mens* being month, *pausis* meaning cessation. But isn't it curious that it sounds like the cessation of men, of sex, of the life-force? And it has consequently become a word to dread. Instead of being associated with a wonderful sense of freedom from the monthly drag and discomfort, it is by tradition associated with the end of a woman's chief function in life; that of childbearing. This is patently absurd today when contraception allows a woman complete control over the number of children she will have, if any at all.

Four pages on in the same dictionary there is another Greek word, 'metamorphosis.' It means transformation, a change of shape which some living things undergo in the natural course of growth. Of course it is referring to creatures like caterpillars and tadpoles, but why can't we adopt the word metamorphosis to explain *our* change of life?

No one knows if the snake feels pain when sloughing off its unwanted skin, or the butterfly panic while battering its way out of the chrysalis, they are natural phases in the life cycle. The menopause is a natural part of our life cycle, like menstruation and giving birth . . . it is just that being humans we have surrounded all the functions with fears, embarrassment and ignorant old wives' tales. In recent years menstruation and birth have been relieved of their mysteries but the menopause is still frequently shrouded in myth.

Young women, and men of all ages, shrug derisively at the irritable behaviour of an older woman; 'menopausal old bitch,' they say uncharitably, regardless of the cause which may be anything from family anxieties to just wet feet. Sympathy is noticeable by its absence, there is an unwritten inference that a woman going through the change of life is about to become a useless member of society.

Even some doctors convey this attitude; a dismissive 'you must expect it at your age' is hardly comforting to a woman whose body is going through a fundamental chemical change. She is made to feel she is wasting his time, that all she can expect from now on is to feel older, uglier and sprout a moustache to boot! And as for sex . . . forget it.

It doesn't have to be like that at all. It *is* another experience and it obviously differs from one body to another, and, like many other bodily functions, a lot depends on the woman's mental attitude and those of the people around her. If it could become less of a taboo subject, an acceptable fact of life along with the others, the shame removed, more women would be able to sail through it without too many difficulties.

From the women I have talked to who have gone through the menopause it seems that the fears are greater than the actuality. None of them could answer the question, 'How long does a hot flush last?' Their memory of discomfort was as vague as the memory of pain after childbirth.

There obviously are moments of embarrassment. Martha Hill had a classic. 'I was driving my Rolls to Ischia, taking my teenage children on holiday and when we got to the South of France I had the most dreadful haemorrhage, it was terribly sudden just as I got out of the car, I had no idea this was the change of life but it was. I just accepted it, it certainly didn't interfere with my sex life, and don't forget that as you get older the inhibitions go.'

On a personal level it was reassuring to hear that the menopause need in no way interfere with a continuing sex life. I had heard nasty rumours of the vagina turning into a dried up prune, rumours that were ruthlessly scotched by an eminent doctor who must remain nameless as he was talking about his own sex life. With unprofessional candour he declared, 'I once had an affair with a woman of fifty-nine and she had the juiciest cunt I have ever come across.' I am sure he meant 'in,' but with expert evidence like that, who's counting?

After that I felt strong enough to do some heavy research and consult the experts. Luckily there is a sudden spate of books on the subject so I was sufficiently well informed to ask a few pertinent questions. I didn't like some of the answers myself but I suppose we all have to face up to it sometime, and like the Girl Guides we were once, be prepared. Or was that the Boy Scouts?

Firstly, it seems on some authorities that menopause is appearing later in life than it used to, perhaps five years later. So that nowadays a woman can expect it somewhere between her fiftieth and fifty-fifth birthday, if she still has such things. The hot flush is still the favourite first signal that the body is about to embark on its hormonal change. It can happen as suddenly as a boy's voice drops in adolescence (a piece of information well worth remembering if any male colleague should notice and find it comical!) The intense blushing occurs usually only on the parts of the body that are exposed, so it may be sensible to wear high-necked and long-sleeved clothes after the first one has caught you by surprise. Dark, absorbent material, preferably, as heavy perspiration can accompany the flush. Personally I have already decided I shall blame it all on booze, a more aceptable excuse until the world is better educated.

There can be at this time an increase in weight, the origin of middle-aged spread, I suppose. For the woman who has kept herself trim the few extra pounds may even be becoming. A French woman once told me that when a woman gets to a certain age she has to choose between her cheeks and her bottom. An unwithered face and neck is worth a couple of inches on the hips.

The woman who has let herself go already may find herself in difficulties. It is easy to get depressed when you don't like your appearance and a lowering of energy is another symptom of the menopause. Neither do laziness and over-indulgence in food or alcohol help at a time like this. Some experts believe that vitamins do; all of them. Vitamins A and D, lots of vitamin C plus all the B complex, and especial emphasis is laid on the benefits of Vitamin E (from wheatgerm) together with a high protein diet. Apparently the thyroid gland needs iodine, the high protein diet helps produce thyroid hormones and the Vitamin E helps absorb the iodine. It also helps alleviate any tendency to restlessness, dizzy spells and heart palpitations.

Quite frankly, laymen as well as doctors have always been divided between the values of vitamins and chemicals as body aids, an additional reason for reading widely on the subject whilst still in the pre-menopausal stage. Some doctors will willingly prescribe hormone-replacement therapy in pill form, but others may have to be coerced. Much recent publicity has been given to possible side-effects, so the choice is yours! A flat refusal of treatment by a doctor is worth the consideration of a second opinion, as this event in one's life can stretch over a two-year period and avoiding unnecessary stress in both public and private life is of topmost priority. There are many brand-names on the market and one needs a doctor who is prepared to spend time on his patients; finding the right hormone-replacement treatment can be just as much a matter of trial and error as finding the right contraceptive pill in youth.

The most noticeable change is going to be in the rhythm of the periods, they will become irregular, there may be more or less bleeding, sometimes they stop altogether. It is extremely important to continue with whatever form of contraception is being used at this time, for until the doctor, whom you should be seeing regularly, gives the go-ahead the danger of pregnancy is still there. It is also worth stating here that many doctors believe that women should find an alternative to the pill by the age of forty.

After the dreary news, the better news. The chief reason for continuing with contraceptives is that many women experience an increase in sex drive during and after the menopause which is basically caused by a slow decrease in the body's production of oestrogen; the ovaries slow down on their egg supply and the womb has no need to provide a potential support station for an egg each month. *But* the body, in its cunning, lovely way, counteracts the loss of oestrogen supply with an increase in androgen, which creates sex drive. So until the ovaries put up their positively final and last production sign, you have to be careful.

Even the clitoris, which may become smaller, compensates by becoming more sensitive, though there may eventually be less secretion from the vagina; some doctors will willingly prescribe a remedy for this but if they are not that enlightened we have all used a jar of petroleum jelly before.

On a cautious level it doesn't sound *too* bad, though there are some horror stories about – one of the nastiest being in Dr David Reuben's *Everything You Always Wanted to Know About Sex But Were Afraid to Ask.* There he states categorically that : '. . . Without oestrogen the quality of being female gradually disappears. The vagina begins to shrivel, the uterus gets smaller, the breasts atrophy, sexual desire often disappears, and the woman becomes completely desexualised. As the oestrogen is shut off a woman comes as close as she can to being a man. Increased facial hair, deepened voice . . .' etc. Is that what Rex Harrison had in mind when he sang 'Why can't a woman be more like a man?' Surely not.

There can be no doubt that the menopause can be a traumatic event in a woman's life, possibly more so to the housewife without a career, whose status depended on her ability to create children; her mystic role is over. The career woman is more likely to seek help if she needs it because she will want to get on with her job.

But it is up to women in all walks of life to educate themselves in order to receive the benefit of medical advances. Magazines, newspapers and books all help increase awareness, so can women by aiding each other through this tricky time. Owning up and discussing treatments could save a lot of distress and a lot of snide remarks from men.

The conspiracy of embarrassment, of silence and ignorance on the subject is enjoined by women as much as men, but with the enormous increase in the numbers of women striving for successful careers and often reaching a peak in them at just this moment it is extremely important that the facts are aired. It would be a shocking, indeed abysmal state of affairs if our society were able to say that Margaret Thatcher was unsuitable to govern because she may be going through the menopause just as she reaches power. Particularly when one considers some of our more recent male prime ministers!

Just as the gays have come out of their closets, we, the New Women, must have the courage to state that we belong to our bodies, that we accept the changes inherent in them and are no longer prepared to suffer a status of forced inferiority. The battery hen mentality as applied to women belongs to the past.

Ruth Halcomb, in her excellent book *Womens' Bodies, Womens' Lives*, covers the subject of the menopause with great authority and wisdom as she does the other horrible events that can overtake one and give cause for self-doubt and fear of loss of sexuality and lovability.

Whilst wishing to heartily endorse and hopefully indeed to practise the resolute maintenance of an active sex life during the menopausal years, I still think love is tremendously important to human beings of both sexes, of all ages. Particularly during crises. And the menopause, when embarked on with insufficient knowledge, must be regarded as a psychological crisis. The relinquishing of the taboo aspect (once associating age in a woman as a disgrace instead of a celebration of her achievements) needs to be shared with lovers and husbands. Women, by bringing the subject into the open and disassociating the symptoms from shame amongst *themselves* are once again able to exercise that self-love that is so important to their success both in their work and private relationships. The change of attitude is coming, many women now look forward to the freedom from the monthly period, especially those who are enjoying a lively sex life. And those are the women who, because they are well informed, and able to handle the situation, receive from the men in their life any extra reassurance needed. It is the ones who wail about their lost youth, who blame their bodies for their inadequacies who force a husband into indifference and a lover to bugger off.

Men need reassurance, too. After all, a woman who fears that her sex life is over is more or less stating that her partner's is as well. Not exactly encouraging for the middle-aged husband who fears impotence (another myth) or for a young man with his urgent sexual needs!

Clairvoyants aside, nobody can foresee the future. Some of the women I talked to have had to face the unpredictable tragedy of losing their young lovers not to other women, but to death. Others have had to cope with loss of a different kind, of a breast or womb. Mastectomy looms high on the list of a woman's fears, especially if she regards her shape as her main source of attraction. One woman, a vital, talented person, a delicious and wicked flirt who had happily pulled young men to her ample bosom for years decided, after her operation, to marry a dull man of her own age. 'I have lived to regret it,' she says sadly, 'it would have been better to have risked rejection and to have lived alone. It was stupid of me but I lost my nerve.'

Another, a woman in her late forties, found a sweetheart of a man, but one loaded with the heavy responsibilities of a cast-off family, a situation which is inhibiting the furthering of her career. A kind, strong and loving woman, she is honest enough to admit that losing a breast probably prevents her from stating her own needs more strenuously. 'Perhaps I would have looked further, wouldn't have considered the situation, but I need love, to give and to receive it.'

A hysterectomy can produce in women similar feelings of female inadequacy and once again doctors and surgeons can be extremely indifferent about what may turn out to be foolish fears, but after an operation when one is in pain it does not help to be told to 'buck up'. Especially if you fear that you are going to lose your sex drive, grow a moustache and never have a fuck again.

Shirley Young ran into all these old wives' tales when she was recovering from her own operation. 'They really should have an adviser in hospitals . . . the things I heard! There was one poor young woman who really thought that after the operation she was going to grow hair on her chest, that her figure would disappear, her voice would drop and that she would lose her boyfriend and become a lesbian. Luckily for her the doctors understood and sent me along as an envoy. I had had the op four days before and was done up like Camille in a floating negligée, my face made up and my hair washed and curled! Then I showed her my fanny and my absolutely tiny scar and she felt a lot better, in fact I did such a good job the doctors had me flashing my fanny for days.'

Shirley would be the first to admit that having a loving partner is of utmost value to an early recovery and that the depression that she managed to avoid would be a hell of a problem to a young childless woman or one married to an unloving man. But as I mentioned earlier, the irrepressible Shirley and Barry were counting the days to try out the statement made by a doctor to another friend of mine . . . 'Don't worry dear, we may have removed the garage but we haven't interfered with the driveway.'

It may sound calculating when one considers this book is about older women and younger men but the indications are that care must be taken when choosing a partner of love. There must be a delicate balance. How much can one ask of another person? Some men are naturally loving and strong, regardless of age, others just can't handle the harshness of physical difficulties.

It is wonderful to be a gaudy, late season butterfly, flitting from one honeyed flower to another. It is imperative to thank the good Lord for each day and try hard to ensure full enjoyment, to take all the medical advice, vitamins and life counselling help one can. To love, live and lust to the best of one's ability and, if necessary, admit that changes have been made. Have had to be made. The one you can't change is human nature, and that includes some adorable young men.

7

THE SOCIAL SIGNIFICANCE

In 1965 Stephen Vizincey wrote a book called *In Praise of Older Women* in which he claimed, 'No girl, however intelligent and warmhearted, can possibly know or feel half as much at twenty as she will at thirty-five.' At the time it seemed that only a few mature, sophisticated men agreed. They were nice men in un-sharp suits with baggy trousers, standard BBC voices and barber shop haircuts. They smile reminiscently, warming themselves on the memories of the women who had been kind to them in their youth . . . those ancient times when nice girls 'didn't'. It was a book about desiring and loving women in an age of, 'Well, I fucked this bird didn't I? Right little darling she was.' It was the age of the mini-skirt, the Pill and the Sarf London accent. To be thirty in those days was practically a criminal offence and to admit it was to become an instant social pariah. And as for Sophie Tucker's adage that 'Life Begins at Forty', they would rather be dead . . . and sadly, a lot of them are.

Thirteen years later America's *Harper's Bazaar* produced a list of their nation's ten most beautiful women, and the top one is Lena Horne, aged sixty. The list goes on to include three in their forties – Elizabeth Taylor, Princess Grace and Diahann Carroll – the rest are in their thirties. A British survey also produced a list of desirable females with Joan Collins topping the lot. Hopefully, it looks like the age of the teeny bopper has been left to the record salesmen. Feminist education and women's magazines can obviously claim a certain amount of credit for this change towards an appreciation of women as growing human beings, so can those scourges of the early feminist movement, the cosmetics and allied beauty industries. Loathe as I am to refer to the vulgarity of the bra-burning incident one must concede that from that fire has risen, if not a phoenix, at least a phalanx of women who are prepared to be responsible for their own lives.

Some women have learned that they have more to offer than the loan of their services in exchange for their keep and a roof for their children. Some haven't and never will, but the ones who have do seem to have acquired a patina, a combination of self-interest and survival that makes them more interesting, generous, intelligent and desirable. So here they are, all grown-up and independent. They have given up the role of lifelong leech to the male. Are they to turn round and become the vampires instead, sucking the youth of the nation dry? Metaphorically speaking you understand.

It was time to turn to an expert again. Glenn Wilson – whose opinions have been useful in earlier chapters – is that rare event, a psychiatrist with a sense of humour. He researches behaviour patterns at the *Institute of Psychiatry*, and is also a consultant for a computer match-making organisation. He reports : 'There is a genuine surplus of older single women and younger men, so it does seem kind of obvious for the two groups to get together but the problem is getting them together. The different bureaux cater for different needs, some of them offer temporary relationships and some are trying to find their clients lifelong partnerships.

'The surplus is due to the usual age differential, older men pairing off with younger women, leaving the young men without young women and older women without older men.'

That triggered off a memory of my son and his friends, all aged nineteen or twenty, bemoaning the lack of available crumpet. They were sitting disconsolately in my kitchen drinking endless cups of instant coffee telling me that the girls that they had been happily exchanging since they were all at school together suddenly changed when they reached eighteen. The girls turned away from their playmates towards blokes with jobs, suits and cars. Looking round the table at half a dozen lads in dirty jeans, T-shirts and motor-cycle boots I thought the girls had a point. Even so I was a bit disconcerted when I discovered that these envied older fellows were all of twenty-five. Some things make you feel older than others.

But back to Glenn Wilson for a glimmer of hope. 'It looks like we could get a reversal of the traditional pattern because the reason for an age discrepancy is nothing to do with relative maturation rates in the sexes, it's a social status thing. What you are getting effectively is a trade-off between the high social status of the man and the physical good looks of the young woman. But as you get progressively more women with high status occupations and interesting accomplishments, then those can be used as a commodity for pairing off with a relatively young man. The social attraction is sufficient to override convention and the more often it happens the weaker the convention will become.

'Of course it can be argued that in socio-biological terms

there is something more natural about high status dominant males trading off with prime-time females,' [I'd felt like a packet of marg. before, now I was beginning to feel a bit rancid], 'as the child-bearing years of a female are between sixteen and thirty-five. From the evolutionary point of view it is important for the males well up the dominance hierarchy to breed with quite a variety of females. And it makes good evolutionary sense for the low ranking males to play by themselves, to masturbate!'

Does that mean that all we, the proud, independent legions of women of forty-plus, can expect are the leftovers?

'Not at all; whilst some men may have to fall back on older women because they can't compete for the younger ones there will always be some who will have a preference for the experience older women have. The salvation of the older woman is probably going to be in the male's exploratory drive, his need for variety and novelty. The fact is the heterosexual male is usually slowed down in his rate of scoring by the restrictions placed on him by his female targets. Men have to "get their rocks off" somewhere, somehow and with fairly steady frequency, and, as the song goes, if women are unavailable "there are knot holes in the floors and there are keyholes in the doors" so the increasing availability of older women must be an advantage to both parties.

'I don't think it is socially irresponsible if it gives them both pleasure though I don't think it is sensible to look for a stable relationship in every case. I don't see very much point in marriage when the woman is old enough to have no prospect or interest in having children. Why complicate your life with legal contracts? If you can accept the social approbation of the association in the first place, why bother? Though why it's there I don't rightly understand. I suppose people think the man is only interested in an older woman for financial reasons and she is interested in him only for physical reasons. But age has little to do with love and when people fall in love it is often the character faults and blemishes – the imperfections, that they love. People often mention the Oedipus (mother/son) complex but it is not a very powerful argument as society is much more paranoid about older male paedophilia – you very seldom hear about female paedophiles. But then the male is more prone to what used to be called deviation – fetish-ims, transvestitism, exhibitionism, voyeurism; all the way back to the lower primates.'

So it looks as if we have the blessing of one influential and worthwhile corner of society and it's comforting to know that not only are we not interfering with Mother Nature's evolutionary process but that we could be doing the world a favour. Just think of all those lower primates out there whom we could save from the perils of rejection by those prime-timers thus preventing them from turning into voyeurs, sadomasochists, necrophiliacs and *frotteurs* (they are the dirty buggers who rub up against you in the tube). What a pity the Women's Voluntary Service have already claimed the initials!

There was one last question.

Where will all the young women go? It would be lovely and frivolous to suggest 'off to older dominant males with their superior genes, everyone' but what *will* be the effect on younger women watching all the good-time old girls rushing around enjoying a career and a lively sex life?

'I think it might give them some hope for the future,' says Glenn, 'they may be a little less desperate to get married and settle down before the age of thirty.

'I think a lot of young girls still think that unless they trap their man while they are young and still have their looks they are going to miss out on everything that life has to offer later on. It will be a good lesson for them to realise that there is plenty of time to develop in their own right, and they may even have more to contribute to a marriage.'

I think that is very sensible. I have noticed in my own daughters' generation a much more relaxed attitude towards commitment, though there is also evidence that this is still very much a class-dominated development. The university graduate and career-orientated girl is bound to be more mobile in her relationships; anxious to explore job possibilities, cities, even continents; she is less likely to rush into early marriage and motherhood than the factory girl who sees her wedding day as an escape from the dull clocking-in routine of life. Though here again the increase of liaisons between older women and younger men could have an effect on the class structure of the future, it being noticeable that the kind of young men attracted to older women in the cross-section I have interviewed are seldom from the conventional middle-classes, with their narrower approval-seeking ambitions. The men are more likely to be what is commonly known as 'rough trade' : not perhaps one of the most flattering forms of reference but very descriptive. It basically means young men with a lot of native charm but lacking in a certain amount of polish; they may have a 'street-talent' like pop musicians, artists or actors, or be just working-class lads with an as yet unformed ambition to improve their status and worldly education. Unlike their middle- or upper-class contemporaries they want to get away from their origins and are not likely to return from a taste of the sophisticated life with a bright, mature woman to the girl from the same street whose horizons are limited by lack of experience. Within ten years the average working-class girl may also find herself seeking a permanent partner later in life and from further afield, she too may begin to look at her man not just as a provider but as a person to grow with.

I'm an inveterate optimist.

Now the current crop of career women in their forties are unlikely to owe much to the post-war explosion of red-brick universities – they are more likely to have achieved their ambitions through that same street-drive and talent that they recognise in their young men. For Molly Parkin meeting Patrick was a welcome return to her roots. 'I found in Patrick something very straightforward, I had had this love affair with middle-class men for a long time and Patrick brought me back to my roots again and that is what I liked about him as much as anything. I had had to go through the middle-class thing to get to where I am now, my first husband even wanted me to have elocution classes, this was in the late Fifties when it was still very important to talk in a particular way. I was crucified with sheer shame and horror every time I entered a room with my first husband, I was dying inside because the vowels weren't quite right. With Patrick I can be myself again.

'Of all the women that I know who have gone with younger men I don't think any of the men are posh, and I don't think I would have fallen for a younger man who was upper-class.'

Being an orphan I always find myself instinctively attracted to men who have made it alone, whose own childhood has included hardship. Pillow-talk of nannies and prep schools makes me decidedly uncomfortable, an inadequacy I have never been able to overcome.

Occasionally the newspapers carry stories of the *Lady Chatterley's Lover* type alliances and doubtless there are many more that never make the headlines, but these are more likely to be between married ladies and their employees and don't really fit in here. Equally one reads of council-house mothers who run off with a neighbour's son, thus depriving the girl next door of her potential quarry, so the focal point of choice, habit and the pattern of the future changes yet again.

From the interviews I have conducted I would suggest that the existing group of older women seek out men of good heart and good humour (though looks and prowess certainly affect their choice), a curious phenomenon in our acquisitive, materialistic world. It is almost as if the recognition of women's rights, the sharing of property, the opportunity to work and the responsibility for their own lives has taught them to be less grasping. Though the information coming in from the United States is distressing, where *men*, lawyers, are using the ground gained by the Women's Movement to attack men financially. The idea of amorality differs from where you are standing but to me, manipulating a woman into claiming millions of dollars from a man whose life she has shared in order to earn a third of the proceeds doesn't sound like progress. Or freedom. But that is America and with our tax system the chances of finding someone worth suing are rare, a bicker over who bought the coffee-grinder is about as far as we are likely to get. So the men in our love-lives are hardly likely to fear for their pockets, they are more likely to be easy-going, true believers in equality with nicely-rounded personalities. A lovely thought for any woman who actually likes men as human beings, who is grateful not to go through the agony of seeing sons and husbands march off to war. But is it going to be a good thing for them?

The Eighties could see, in the West at least, a generation of bright, forceful women of achievement attached to a generation of young men only too happy to discard the traditional male role. Fine for the bright women – society will at least be harnessing the other half of its intellectual energy – but what about all those adorable young men who would rather learn to live (even to the point of ignoring their evolutionary role) rather than strive to live? If a man would rather be in bed driving a woman wild instead of playing macho games in a car on the motorways, what would happen to Fords, Leylands and the garage proprietors?

If personality, rather than diamonds, are to become a girl's best friend, what will happen to de Beers, Hatton Garden and the miners?

Insurance policies, based on the fact that the wage-earning man dies first, will become redundant as the easy-going male relieves himself of the stress role . . . what price Prudential shares then?

Of course this is fantasy – I doubt if we shall ever see processions of younger women carrying placards bearing the slogan 'Down With Older Women' (too many of us too willing for a start) – men and women will always beget together at sometime in their lives. But it is a marvellous thought that we, the older women, disregarded for centuries, might be the real revolutionaries, changing the structure of society from within.

And using its very weapon too. Dr Charlotte Woolf, truly a woman of this century and almost its age (she is the author of *An Older Love* and *Bisexuality*) approves of and endorses this fantastic theory. 'There is a revolution

133

going on inside women that has created a New Woman. The old cliché of the 'feminine' woman is dying and from the angle of the male-dominated society this is the most dangerous revolution in 2000 years. This is the moment of the woman and they need no more proof, they are truly part of the evolution of society at a time when the other attempts at change through Socialism and Communism have failed because both those conceptions looked at people from the outside.

'I am against female chauvinism as much as I am against male chauvinism and there is a danger that now women have this new sense of power they will mistake independence with mastery. There is the chance that the older woman, particularly the one who has found her self-assurance through an individual quality, as opposed to the organisation of the Women's Liberation Movement, might be attracted to the young man because he is weaker than herself. Women's Liberation has changed, or is changing, men too, and it is likely that the new, self-confident, powerful woman will be more attracted to younger men because it is they who have shed the clichés, they who are far more open to new ideas; the men of her age are far more inclined to still be stamped by the attitudes of past generations.

'The change in men is also evolutionary and probably far more difficult than anything women have experienced. They, the women, have become stronger, they are moving upwards in all aspects of society, but men, in the stupid, conventional sense of what was acceptable, are being forced into a state of uncertainty.

'I have thrown out from my mind and vocabulary the words 'feminine' and 'masculine' because they are both artefacts, inventions that have made the male and female into something artificial that serves the purpose of society.

'I think that recently the biological age of women has disappeared, after all ageing is a process of the mind, it is a psychosomatic attitude. One can see children, young people, who are old, closed mentally, and other people who remain totally aware all their lives. There are women whose erotic age will always be twenty or twenty-five – we are all ages, categories are nonsense.

'But if, through the new woman, the development of the male now goes 'feminine' into perceptiveness, sensitivity and less aggression, I personally believe he is becoming a stronger man.'

Meeting Dr Woolf was an exhilarating experience because she demonstrates more than anyone the power and charm of the lively, questing mind. She was for me living proof that women, as well as men, can go on learning and contributing long after that dread crisis of arriving at the age of forty. Of course the appearance changes eventually, subtly, but to have put those extra thirty years between forty and seventy to good use, sexually, mentally and, forgive the pomposity, even for the benefit of society, can't be all bad, can it?

8

THE YOUNG MEN'S TALES

Manners maketh woman too, so it seemed only fair to allow the young men their say . . . and very illuminating it was. To judge by their statements and recorded adventures the age gap is bridged considerably more often than the world suspects, and, if I may be so indiscreet, infinitely more often than many husbands detect!

The bored and lonely housewives are, apparently, not the myth I thought they were. The tales of young vacuum-cleaner salesmen being greeted at the front door by stark naked ladies; young house-painters shinning down drain pipes at the unexpected sound of the key in the door, and the one about the lad who leaped up the area steps and into the husband's still-warm taxi with all his clothes tucked underneath his arm (the driver went solemnly round the corner where he had to stop, get out of the cab and roll all over the pavement laughing) are all too authentically and hilariously told to be untrue. Besides that, I know the narrators and they have no need to tell lies.

But as I said at the beginning, this book is not aimed at errant wives.

My research took me into many conversations with men of all ages and the subject was taken up with enthusiasm, tenderness and warmth. An elderly man in his seventies spoke meltingly of the woman he had met when he was twenty-five, a woman twenty years his senior who had shown him the art of loving, a gift he had shared and enjoyed all his life ... and was quite anxious to continue sharing. Many middle-aged men recalled the women who had been generous enough to encourage them in the days when youths were more callow than they are today, and young men spoke of their fear of making an approach, something I had not suspected.

There were contrasts, too, of class, careers, and remorse for opportunities missed. Having an elegant lunch with a father and son one day the man was ruing the fate of his own age group (mine). When *he* was young it was unthinkable to make a pass at a senior man's wife and now, in his forties, he finds he is missing out again; his attractive female contemporaries are turning to younger men. The son, an incredibly pretty eighteen-year-old was shocked; straight out of public school he was indignantly asserting the pleasures of girls his own age. A couple of bottles of wine and two hours of beguiling and amusing conversation later, his harsh views softened, and from the warm farewell kiss he gave me I felt sure that he would regard the next older woman he met in a different light. Well, it would be a shame to let him waste his life like his father, wouldn't it?

It must be accepted that not all young men are attracted to older women even in fantasy (hosts of them are more concerned with finding a Mrs Right than a Mrs Robinson) but throughout these interviews, both formal and informal, one fact comes shining through ... those that are really *like* women. They like them to talk to as well as to make love to, and the words that ran through all their conversations describing their relationships were : interesting, funny and *sensual*. They have mostly played stud at some time in their lives (that exploratory drive again). They have certainly experienced sex with all age groups and they have all been accused of, and thought seriously about, the Oedipus complex. The sophisticated ones have looked around, shrugged their shoulders, and agreed with the world that all love is blind; the others, usually younger, struggle, sometimes flounder, and occasionally flee for their lives. They have a lot to work out and that is their right as human beings.

As I said, I talked to a lot of men. Some had loved their mothers, some had had no mothers, some were neurotic and some were easy on themselves; but the ones I found most pitiful were the grown men who regard women as something to burnish their egos, a mere decoration for the end of their cock, the ones who had never learned to enjoy women's company.

In the end I thought it best to let the men tell their own stories and experiences.

I chose a random four. They all spoke with great honesty, though once again some of them wished their names to be changed for personal reasons. *I* think their stories are very revealing, some worrying and some encouraging, they are probably even eternal, but then, even I haven't been around that long. Travelling hopefully I would say there is a possibility of a change in men's attitudes towards women, an opposite to the male chauvinist pig so reviled in the Seventies. For our survival into the Eighties maybe we should ask, 'Are there any more at home like these ?'

Let's look, listen and learn.

Marcus is a tall, good-looking bachelor of twenty-four, he was brought up 'in care' after his parents' divorce, and works in the film industry.

'I first fell in love with an older woman when I was eighteen, I had lost my virginity only the year before . . . to a girl of fourteen. She had seduced me!

'I had had crushes on women, mostly because they are better company and can talk about things – girls only want to go to the pub or discos – but I had never been able to break the ice. I'm basically shy and knew I couldn't get away with the ham line, the silly chat-up, but one evening I was in the studio bar and Fran came in. I had seen her around for a couple of months but she was much too grand for me to talk to until this day when the conversation turned to the subject of my father, who is very admired in the business. I was able to introduce myself and we started to talk. I idolise my father and I love films so suddenly we had a lot in common and we went on to the pub and then home together quite naturally.

'Yes, I was horrified that first morning, lying next to a woman sixteen years older than me who had taken all her make-up off. I thought, "Good grief – all those nineteen-year-olds I could have pulled", but by the time she was dressed and had put her make-up on I was head over heels in love. I felt great but dreadfully embarrassed when we got to the studio, everybody knew, it went round like wild-fire and I was only the mailboy! I had to go into every single office, including hers. There was one comfort; I was now established as a heterosexual and it stopped the gays making passes at me. I was terrified to go back to the bar, and she was shy too, but I sent her a drink, she accepted it and we went on from there.

'She taught me a lot sexually because I had a lot to

learn, and one of the things was how to be her escort. We ran into all those comments like, "Is this your son?" and that threw me at first. I was still running around in tank-tops, but one day, when we had a very important date, I went out and bought my first suit. I had to change my image to suit her as there was no way a grand lady executive could change hers to suit mine. When I arrived at her door to pick her up she was thrilled to bits.

'I have always been a romantic, I love to spoil women and she was more appreciative than any girl could have been.

'Ironically, what had begun through my father ended with his return. Fran felt she couldn't work with my father and see me, it was too damaging to her career. I never found out if there was another relationship, but I was heartbroken. So I got promoted from mailboy and became super-stud all round the office, every little bird thought that I must be good to have pulled an older woman. It took me a year to get over it, I was sick of silly flirts, but I had had enough of older women so I started to go to gay bars just because I missed some level of conversation, I preferred their company without becoming gay.

'So I moved on; by the time I was twenty I had discovered that the twenty-eight- to thirty-year-olds weren't all that interesting . . . and then I met Lisa, who was forty-two. She was voluptuous, plump actually, and clever and cultured, I met her when I was working in a summer show and she pulled me. With her I learned how to love someone and respect them at the same time, we looked after each other, had fun, and did positive things like going to exhibitions, concerts, old houses, auctions. She talked about the things that interested her and taught me about them. She gave me the drive to work at my career.

'We were together for eighteen months but in the end all we had in common was sex. She was a sexual athlete, she wanted more and I lost interest.

'In the end I behaved like a shit and fucked both her daughters. And I had wanted to marry her.

'I am still hung up on older women, if I meet an attractive woman I can talk to her but I can't talk to young girls, and at the moment it is a problem I don't want to resolve as I have just fallen in love with another older woman.'

Bill is a Canadian, the owner of the most distinguished voice in advertising. Aged forty-two, married three times and an orphan.

'I was twelve years old and as tall as I am now, that's six foot. I had been sent out to foster homes three times and sent back three times. I was at this new college in Ontario finding my way around, not exactly delinquent but quite sure I didn't want to be out on the fields playing ball games with the boys, when I walked into the kitchens and saw this great Grecian beauty bending over doing the dish-washing and I *knew* that was where the action was. My problem was that I had found the answer to life, but how could I get to it? So I offered to help with the washing-up. She was thirty-two. I spent a lot of time in her bedroom, training, when everyone else was out on the fields *doing* things.

'By the time I was thirteen we were both thrown out but I was sure enough of myself to take on eighteen-year-olds. I was tall and could lie about my age. That Grecian taught me a lot.

'Well, round the world and a bust-up marriage later; I was thirty-two years old, snatching a living where I could and I met this woman of forty-eight. It was instant lightning. A friend had taken me to her flat, it was so grand, she was in the fashion business, and all the chairs seemed so fragile. By then I was heavy as well as six foot and terrified to sit on one of those Regency chairs. When I found one I could manage I just looked at her. She was so sensual, she had such style and class.

'My friend, a very well-mannered Englishman, got embarrassed and left. Now I was a great big North-American Jewish schmuck, I had done a bit of acting and a bit of other things, and Danielle was an elegant woman of the world who used to be taken out to dinner at all the smart places. So I asked her to the movies, she was so surprised she said yes and we sat in the back row and necked. She told me she felt seventeen.

'The word I have for her always is gorgeous. She was gorgeous.

'I moved in when she asked me, and the rumour soon got about that I was living with some old broad, so I took her out to the Queen's Elm, a pub where I was known, and everyone was round her like bees round a honey pot. They all wanted to know who this fascinating dame was. "That's the old broad," I told them.

'The great thing about her was that she was never embarrassed about being with me, she introduced me so naturally to her friends. She was gracious and I was so *proud* of her.

'I *like* women – they are funnier than girls, they have an instinctive sense of humour. There was a time when she tried to turn me into a tailor's dummy, she took me off to Selfridges and got me these blazers and things, but after

142

four days I looked exactly the same; as if I had slept in them. I just don't have the figure. So she looked at me and said, "Bill, *your* taste is abominable, you can only dress in black or white and with your habits it had better be black, just always buy expensive things, they stand a chance." I've kept to that advice ever since.

'She educated me, she taught me French, and she taught me the difference between sexuality and sensuality. She taught me how to use the right knives and forks and in exchange I taught her how to smell phonies. Sometimes when her smart fashion friends got smashed they would try and corner me in the kitchen, make dates for "tea". I couldn't stand that, I'm a one to one man, I don't mess around, I couldn't bear to see her insulted, so I showed her how to be street-corner smart.

'She found it difficult to believe that I was in love with her, that I wanted to ball her all the time. Sometimes when she had guests, and I thought they were all full of horse-shit I'd just drag her into the hallway and give it to her *there and then*. She never really understood that she didn't need negligées and glamour and she had this fear of younger women that would make her introduce them to me. I'd talk to them for a while, wait till I saw her leave the room, then catch her in the kitchen or drag her into the bedroom, and tell her, "It's you I want you silly old bag." I used to tease her to bring it into the open, but balling her wasn't to reassure her, I wanted to.

'But other times we made love with words. I was reading everything I could, John Donne and Rimbaud, she encouraged my eagerness to learn and experiment with metaphysics, and with her physical sensuality we met in the middle.

'I only think of her as sensual. Until you asked me it

never occurred to me, but I suppose there is a difference, skin; an older woman is softer, but what was between us was right between the eyes. I always look at women's mouths, if the mouth is working then everything else will be in conjunction, though the sound, the voice, is important too.

'Our affair lasted two years. Then she had an hysterectomy and seemed to change completely. I became the enemy. I tried to tell her, "You will always be you," but she became full of fear. I was just beginning to work and she looked into the future and saw a successful man in his forties tied to a woman of fifty-five. She became very French and very practical and married a man of her own age.

'It was very hurtful at first even though I could understand it intellectually. I spent three years hiding, stripping myself, studying metaphysics. I wrote a song about her. Then I came out into life and went on with my blunders, massive ones. But I learned to work and I learned to make money. I still miss her dreadfully. I seek the qualities in others but don't find them; if I wake up in the morning with a woman under thirty-five, I have nothing to say to her, just an awful anxiety to get rid of her.

'If lovers don't laugh in the morning they've got nowhere to go.'

Robin is an athletic, dark horse of a bachelor, aged thirty-two, brought up by conventional parents in comfortable, colonial style. He is a director of an advanced technology magazine.

'I think people of my age are dealing with a more complicated society than ever before, we have grown up in a confusing world of changing standards. My boyhood was spent amongst people of the old guard, regular servicemen stationed in South-east Asia. We had servants, cars, boats and beaches galore, we took our elders for granted but respected them, particularly their wives. Good manners were absolutely essential out there; the familiarity, the breaking down of class barriers through pop music and fashion, hadn't even begun in our carefully maintained hierarchy.

'And that is where my luck began. My father's business and social life forced me into contact with a lot of bored wives. Polite conversation would reveal that they knew nothing of the island I loved so passionately and with my youthful enthusiasm I would escort them all over the place. The husbands were delighted, I was far too young to be a threat and they were right, I was too young to even know that extra-marital adventures existed. My very naïvety contributed to my success because I learned to get on with women naturally.

'Then my eighteenth birthday coincided with the opening of an exhibition my mother was organising, it was a very glamorous affair, and that night I met my first Mrs Robinson. I had seen her before on the beach where I taught water-skiing. All the boys were after her daughter and I thought I was scoring because I taught her. It was all very formal : she asked me about the presents I had received. I told her the list, and then because I was drunk and feeling bold I told her that the one present I wanted I couldn't ask my parents for. I said, "I want to screw the arse off you !"

' "Shall I slap your face now or save it till later?" was her only comment, and two days later she rang me to hire the boat to go to the races on another island. She brought a picnic and we watched the start of the race. She behaved impeccably, a discreet finger up and down my spine, a loose holding of hands. I was very shy but she suggested we leave the grand party and take our picnic to a tiny island, not much more than a large rock, where she set the food and wine out elegantly. Then she stripped off completely and ran into the sea. Of course I had to follow, we frolicked for a while and then came out and made love.

'Whatever fears a man has disappear when a woman makes a possibility certain, and after that age disappears, a horny man is a horny man whatever his age, and I was a very fit, horny man. Until then I had only been with girls of my own age and it had all been guesswork. It was the sureness of what she wanted ... out of her own sensuous feelings, the calculated and direct way she stated her demands ... "Not so fast, and yes, oh yes," ... it was immensely flattering, and I remember my erection getting bigger and bigger because she verbalised, as the Americans would say.

'Afterwards she was the first person ever to ask me to "stay inside", before that, with girls, we had both been too embarrassed and unknowing to know what to do.

'She was the most sympathetic person I have ever known, she gave me every aspect of her loveliness, we did things together and she had the same enthusiasm as a girl even though she was thirty-nine. And she never gushed, or pretended; our social scene made our paths cross a lot, I had to escort girls, but she was so controlled and adjusted, and I now think it was her skill that stopped me falling in love with her. The secret meetings and sudden opportunities were very thrilling against that formal society. Eventually it slowed down, at that age I wanted lots of women, and she became a fond friend.

'She taught me to treat women in a fun-loving way, to

grasp the potential for laughter in women. My father had always treated them as a different species, creatures to be formal and courteous to – I learned to enjoy them.

'But I made some silly mistakes; there were lots of wives in their early forties with voluptuous bodies and sexy faces and I felt I had to have them all. It all got a bit too hot and I ended up scared of those pretty, cut-glass, snobbish Army ladies; once you get through their mental hymen they behave like animals, scratching and biting, and they also become very possessive. It was time to move on to Europe to rediscover all I had learned.

'In some ways a good relationship with an older woman spoils you for contemporaries, or girls of a suitably conventional age, but I don't agree that a preference for mature women is an Oedipal thing. Surely that would be a hang-up, and a hang-up would prevent a young man getting an erection, and that's the last thing either party wants.

'And I genuinely find older women so *fanciable*. Yes, I have registered skin defects, marks, but they made no discouragement whatsoever. I think the kind of men who insist on that sort of perfection, the *Mayfair* or *Playboy* image wouldn't go near an older woman, and I wonder if those sorts of men ever get satisfaction from any woman? The best thing they can do is buy themselves a blow-up doll and have a hand job – no human being is ever going to come up to their expectations.

'Now I am looking to the future, I have started to think about decisions like marriage and a family. As a man I feel assured now, my maturity has been achieved under the umbrella of my older mistresses. My determination now is to work towards taking on the challenge of my contemporaries, I feel that perhaps a bit of me has become mentally flabby, in fact at the moment I can't deal with anything but young birds, certainly not women of my own age. In a way I am looking for a partner to whom I can pass on all that I have learned, I seek the chemistry and I am trying to acquire the mental muscle to deal with the situation. But I haven't closed my options ... if I had to marry right now it would be with an older woman.'

Barry is a short, wiry, interior decorator, thirty-three, married once with two children, and brought up with three brothers by his widowed mother.

'The fact is *all* men fancy women before they fancy birds. If you take the whole sex thing most boys' first sexual encounter is a wank and it isn't going to be over the little girls in the classroom, it is over film stars and pin-ups, and it progresses to the barmaid in the pub, the boss's secretary or even a teacher, but always someone more mature.

'My first real affair with an older woman happened to me when I was sixteen, I was an apprentice house painter and it was my first job. She was the lady of the house, about thirty-five and I fancied her like mad. I had lost my virginity when I was twelve (with an older girl ... she was fourteen) and this was my very first lustful affair. My role was strictly stud, but I felt so proud, pulling a well-fancied married lady, mind you she had probably pulled me, but it went on for months and only finished because I was given the choice of her or the sack from my job, I was going missing too often.

'The really exciting thing about her was being able to make love with nothing on and the chance to try out all the positions I instinctively knew were possible, it certainly beat having a knee-trembler on a frosty night. In those days girls of my own age were a bit inhibited and you wouldn't get one giving you a blow job or letting you go down on her. But by the time I had gone through the *Kama Sutra* with my lady I got bored because there was no other development for the relationship.

'When I was younger it was difficult to have a real affair with an older woman because they were embarrassed to be seen walking down the street with you. Being a house painter there were plenty of opportunities for fucking, but the social stigma, like the lack of money to take them out and the difference in life-styles, was just too much to deal with. In those days older women were into ballroom dancing; rock 'n' roll nights were youth nights and she wouldn't want to walk around with a teenager and his spotty friends, and in any case your friends would have thought you were mad.

'In the *early* Sixties you crept in, had your screw and buggered off; the secrecy, whether because of the husband, the children or what the neighbours might think, prevented any real relationship growing in any direction. Also, at that age you're a bit insensitive, you just want anything that moves, and with the girls of my age it took so long to get their knickers down, you'd have had the horn for hours, after all that groping and pretending you're not, you would just grab it and that was that. There was no comparing the older woman's sexual abandon with what you could get.

'I went back to my own age group partly because they were available and partly because older women just didn't fancy young men then. I married, then lived with several girls, but looking back I can honestly say I don't think I learned anything more from that first encounter with an older woman than I would have anyway. I think a sexual being doesn't need to be taught and a non-sexual being cannot learn.

'If you fancy someone you don't relate to their age, only to their sensuality or whatever it is about them that attracts you. Most fellas will own up amongst themselves to having lusted after older women, perhaps someone round the office, but they don't get much encouragement.

'The current switchover has come from the women themselves, *they* have changed, the social embarrassment has started to wane. I now live with a woman a lot older than me, twelve years in fact, and I know a lot of young men that tried to chat her up and didn't succeed. I also know a lot of others who think she is a bit old for me but who would probably die for half a chance to get their leg over. It's funny really, society is still shocked even though it is changing, it is the male ego that is offended, they think that if she has chosen one young man she must be available to others, it is a challenge to them.

'My lady and I were good friends long before we became lovers, in fact I was her confidante, it took me a long time to persuade her that I had fancied her all along. She kept insisting that she was too old for me but we have been living happily together now for two years.

'Once a woman gets over the paranoia of the years difference it just doesn't matter at all. If this affair finishes, God forbid, I think it is more than likely that I would look for another older woman, I tend to fancy them. It's not an Oedipal thing, though, because I don't like being mothered, or wived for that matter. When I was younger I did the breadwinner role, first for my family of brothers then with a wife and children and I don't want it any more, I prefer the equality that comes with living with an older woman. What I like about the relationship is the lack of competitiveness between us, there is less game playing and scoring off each other, and more mutual support; she's more mature, grown-up. She has probably done it all before and seen how destructive it is.

'Sexually the older woman is better on the one-night-stand level but once you are into a relationship the age thing is irrelevant and the sex is as good as the love you have for each other.

'Of course I am aware of the age signs – older skin, stretch-marks, you couldn't not be, but they just don't bother me. Older women's *bodies* have character as well as their faces, those young, firm tits that women think we all yearn for have little or no movement and very little sensitivity, the nipples that respond best are usually on women who have had children. If only women would remember that not all young girls have perfect bodies.

'I don't look ahead and worry about any health problems she may have in the future like the menopause, anyhow she's as strong as an ox and will probably far outlive me. I'm not the sort of person to think about "what if, or when" – when we first started she wasted a lot of energy about how it is going to end and when, but if the relationship grows and continues, I expect I shan't notice her ageing. It's a bit like watching your children grow up, you don't notice as they get taller.

'Over the years friends have stopped noticing the difference between us, even strangers take our togetherness as a natural thing, she has grown in confidence and has become less self-conscious. It's obvious that she is not a dolly bird, they know she is older than me but she's glamorous and looks great in the gear she wears. I make an effort not to look like a teenager, I have let my hair grow because she complains that I look too young with it short.

'If there is a problem it is that she is a terrible flirt, she always has been, but she does get dreadfully jealous if I pay attention to anyone, especially if they are younger, because although she knows I fancy older women she still feels threatened. The insecurity of the older woman could, if not made allowances for, fuck up the relationship and probably does in quite a few cases. It's funny really because young men are much more nervous trying to pull an older woman than one of their own age, because amongst their own group they are likely to be the more experienced. The reason they fancy mature women is because of their grandness and sophistication, they admire them and consider them to be better than themselves and consequently beyond their reach.

'One of the wonderful things about having an affair with an older woman is her social aplomb, you can arrange to meet her anywhere and not worry too much if you are delayed. She won't be standing outside the pub too scared to go in on her own, and if someone makes the wrong remark she needs no defending, she can handle situations.

'One of the disadvantages in my case is that she has had more time to collect a long string of ex-lovers . . . I've had to learn social aplomb too!'

FINALE

It was a mistake to have interviewed the young men last. It brought back a flood of memories of opportunities lost through my own late development. To think it took me all those years to realise what nice, gentle, available sweethearts men are. As I said in the Introduction, we *can* learn from our errors, and I hope you will learn from mine. One of the young men sought me out later, alas not for that, but to point out the fundamental difference between older men and older women. 'The reason why men have always been able to pull birds over the years,' he told me, 'is that they never consider themselves old, no man ever considers himself past it. Now women are beginning to have the same attitude, women's thinking has always influenced society though they had to use men to get what they wanted.'

Realistically, the older woman cannot and never will be a threat to the younger woman, but her penchant for younger men and her freedom to indulge it *will* influence the future. The men who eventually return to their contemporaries will be better lovers and more understanding people.

As Lynda Trapnell so succinctly put it, 'It's the chicks of the future who are the lucky ones . . . they will find their older men (our young ones) just as interesting sexually as we find them now.'

Long live sex!

So the change of life towards the end of the twentieth century is indeed a change for both men and women. We all have much to learn from one another. And like all new systems we need a few laws laid out for us, so I drew up a couple of sets of rules. No offence intended, but the one for the fellas is longest. They have a longer road ahead!

CONDUCT BECOMING TO YOUNG MEN IN SEARCH OF OLDER WOMEN

Make sure you have half a chance before making an approach; she is experienced enough to tell you to fuck off.

Praise her personality, clothes and style before you start on her looks.

Avoid all age references; hers and particularly yours. Being born after the war is no particular sin but it is nothing to boast about either.

Don't turn up to meet her in dirty jeans and running shoes.

Let her buy you a drink if offered, do not insult her hard-won independence.

Be extremely courteous, open doors for her, light her cigarettes, and so on, she is used to it and will not think you are a creep.

Avoid playing games with mates: darts, pool, and so on.

Avoid playing games with younger birds, especially the kind mentioned above, it puts you at a disadvantage.

If, having scored; take your cue at the next meeting from her. There could be boss or husband trouble.

BUY HER THIS BOOK!

Relax about your age.

Don't ask his.

Let him know you fancy him, he's the shy one. If he chickens, pull his friend. It's a man you're after.

Allow him to call the taxi even if you are paying. Or get on the bus with him. Offer him a drink. It shows you are equals.

Keep on taking the vitamins.

And everything else, at any time he offers.

Don't buy him expensive presents.

Don't wait more than an hour.

Keep him away from your friends.

And if he falls in love, start running. You can always use your age as an excuse if you falter on the way!

Also in Hamlyn Paperbacks

Susie Orbach

FAT IS A FEMINIST ISSUE

The book that begins the diet revolution

Throw away your diet sheets, stop starving yourself
. . . and still lose weight. Those words may seem like
an impossible dream for the millions of women
caught in the diet-binge-diet trap. But they spell out
the message of this book.

Fat is a Feminist Issue is an *anti-diet* book. Forget
calorie-counting, forbidden foods and the tyranny
of the scales – in this practical self-help manual,
Susie Orbach explains how women can liberate
themselves from feelings of guilt and shame about
food and fatness. She explains *why* women get fat,
why they regain weight after dieting . . . and how they
can learn to stabilize their weight.

Already she's shown thousands of women how to
beat the compulsive eating syndrome. Now let her
show you.

Donald Norfolk

THE STRESS FACTOR

Strategies for survival

Every day each of us is under stress. Domestic crisis, competition at work, anxiety about the future can wreck a healthy life. The symptoms are fatigue, illness . . . and even premature death. But stress is also a vital, positive force – properly controlled it will enrich our lives.

In **The Stress Factor** relaxation expert Donald Norfolk shows us how to recognise the enemy and turn it to our advantage. He points out the danger signals of stress overload and puts forward techniques to avoid it.

We *can* modify our behaviour. We *can* control stress. We *can* harness stress to aid success. The choice is ours.

Prices and postage and packing rates shown below were correct at the time of going to press.

FICTION

All prices shown are exclusive of postage and packing

GENERAL FICTION

☐ THE CAIN CONSPIRACY	J. M. Simmel	£1.20
☐ THE AFFAIR OF NINA B	J. M. Simmel	£1.20
☐ HMS BOUNTY	John Maxwell	£1.00
☐ SEARCHING FOR CALEB	Anne Tyler	95p
☐ CELESTIAL NAVIGATION	Anne Tyler	95p
☐ THE ENTREPRENEUR	I. G. Broat	£1.00
☐ THE SOUNDS OF SILENCE	Judith Richards	£1.00
☐ TY-SHAN BAY	Raoul Templeton Aundrews	95p
☐ A SEA CHANGE	Lois Gould	80p
☐ THE PLAYERS	Gary Brandner	95p
☐ RIDDLE	Dan Sherman	90p
☐ THE PECOS MANHUNT (Western)	Matt Chisholm	75p
☐ MR. FITTON'S COMMISSION	Showell Styles	85p
☐ CRASH LANDING	Marc Regan	95p

CRIME/THRILLER

☐ THE TWO FACES OF JANUARY	Patricia Highsmith	95p
☐ THOSE WHO WALK AWAY	Patricia Highsmith	95p
☐ A GAME FOR THE LIVING	Patricia Highsmith	95p
☐ THE BLUNDERER	Patricia Highsmith	95p
☐ THE TREMOR OF FORGERY	Patricia Highsmith	80p
☐ STRAIGHT	Steve Knickmeyer	80p
☐ FIVE PIECES OF JADE	John Ball	85p
☐ IN THE HEAT OF THE NIGHT	John Ball	85p
☐ THE EYES OF BUDDHA	John Ball	85p
☐ THE COOL COTTONTAIL	John Ball	80p
☐ JOHNNY GET YOUR GUN	John Ball	85p
☐ FLETCH	Gregory Mcdonald	90p
☐ CONFESS, FLETCH	Gregory Mcdonald	90p
☐ THE TRIPOLI DOCUMENTS	Henry Kane	95p
☐ THE EXECUTION	Oliver Crawford	90p
☐ TIME BOMB	James D. Atwater	90p
☐ THE SPECIALIST	Jasper Smith	85p
☐ KILLFACTOR FIVE	Peter Maxwell	85p
☐ ROUGH DEAL	Walter Winward	85p
☐ THE SONORA MUTATION	Albert J. Elias	85p

ROMANCE

☐ ROYAL FLUSH	Margaret Irwin	£1.20
☐ THE BRIDE	Margaret Irwin	£1.20
☐ THE PROUD SERVANT	Margaret Irwin	£1.25
☐ THE GAY GALLIARD	Margaret Irwin	£1.25
☐ THE STRANGER PRINCE	Margaret Irwin	£1.25
☐ DAUGHTER OF DESTINY	Stephanie Blake	£1.25
☐ FLOWERS OF FIRE	Stephanie Blake	£1.00
☐ BLAZE OF PASSION	Stephanie Blake	£1.20
☐ MYSTIC ROSE	Patricia Gallagher	£1.20
☐ CAPTIVE BRIDE	Johanna Lindsey	£1.00
☐ A PIRATE'S LOVE	Johanna Lindsey	£1.20
☐ ROSELYNDE	Roberta Gellis	£1.20
☐ ALINOR	Roberta Gellis	£1.20
☐ JOANNA	Roberta Gellis	£1.25
☐ GREEN GIRL	Sandra Heath	80p

SCIENCE FICTION

☐ THE OTHER LOG OF PHILEAS FOGG	Philip José Farmer	80p
☐ GRIMM'S WORLD	Vernor Vinge	75p
☐ A TOUCH OF STRANGE	Theodore Sturgeon	85p
☐ THE SILENT INVADERS	Robert Silverberg	80p
☐ THE SEED OF EARTH	Robert Silverberg	80p
☐ CRITICAL THRESHOLD	Brian Stableford	75p
☐ THE FLORIANS	Brian M. Stableford	80p
☐ FURY	Henry Kuttner	80p
☐ MUTANT	Henry Kuttner	90p
☐ HEALER	F. Paul Wilson	80p
☐ CAGE A MAN	F. M. Busby	75p
☐ JOURNEY	Marta Randall	£1.00
☐ THE WARRIORS OF DAWN	M. A. Foster	£1.10
☐ THE GAMEPLAYERS OF ZAN	M. A. Foster	£1.25

HORROR/OCCULT

☐ ISOBEL	Jane Parkhurst	£1.00
☐ THE HOWLING	Gary Brandner	85p
☐ RETURN OF THE HOWLING	Gary Brandner	85p
☐ SPIDERS	Richard Lewis	80p
☐ RETURN OF THE LIVING DEAD	John Russo	80p
☐ DYING LIGHT	Evan Chandler	85p
☐ RATTLERS	Joseph L. Gilmore	85p
☐ LOCUSTS	Guy N. Smith	85p

FILM/TV TIE IN

☐ WUTHERING HEIGHTS	Emily Brontë	80p
☐ STAND ON IT	Stroker Ace	95p
☐ THE ROSE MEDALLION	James Grant	90p

NON-FICTION

- [ ] THE HAMLYN BOOK OF
      CROSSWORDS 1   60p
- [ ] THE HAMLYN BOOK OF
      CROSSWORDS 2   60p
- [ ] THE HAMLYN BOOK OF
      CROSSWORDS 3   60p
- [ ] THE HAMLYN BOOK OF
      CROSSWORDS 4   60p
- [ ] THE HAMLYN FAMILY GAMES
      BOOK   Gyles Brandreth   75p
- [ ] LONELY WARRIOR (War)   Victor Houart   85p
- [ ] BLACK ANGELS (War)   Rupert Butler   £1.00
- [ ] THE BEST OF DIAL-A-RECIPE   Audrey Ellis   80p
- [ ] THE SUNDAY TELEGRAPH PATIO
      GARDENING BOOK   Robert Pearson   80p
- [ ] THE COMPLETE TRAVELLER   Joan Bakewell   £1.50
- [ ] RESTORING OLD JUNK   Michèle Brown   75p
- [ ] FAT IS A FEMINIST ISSUE   Susie Orbach   85p
- [ ] AMAZING MAZES 1   Michael Lye   75p
- [ ] GUIDE TO THE CHANNEL ISLANDS   Janice Anderson and
                                           Edmund Swinglehurst   90p
- [ ] THE STRESS FACTOR   Donald Norfolk   90p
- [ ] WOMAN × TWO   Mary Kenny   90p
- [ ] THE HAMLYN BOOK OF
      BRAINTEASERS AND
      MINDBENDERS   Ben Hamilton   85p
- [ ] THE HAMLYN CARTOON
      COLLECTION 2   70p
- [ ] WORLD WAR 3   edited by Shelford Bidwell £1.25
- [ ] THE HAMLYN BOOK OF
      AMAZING INFORMATION   80p

KITCHEN LIBRARY

- [ ] MIXER AND BLENDER COOKBOOK   Myra Street   80p
- [ ] HOME BAKED BREADS AND CAKES   Mary Norwak   75p
- [ ] EASY ICING   Marguerite Patten   85p
- [ ] HOME MADE COUNTRY WINES   40p
- [ ] COMPREHENSIVE GUIDE TO DEEP
      FREEZING   40p
- [ ] COUNTRY FARE   Doreen Fulleylove   80p
- [ ] HOME PRESERVING AND BOTTLING   Gladys Mann   80p
- [ ] WINE MAKING AT HOME   Francis Pinnegar   80p

All these books are available at your local bookshop or newsagent, or can be ordered direct from the publisher. Just tick the titles you want and fill in the form below.

NAME...

ADDRESS ....

....

Write to Hamlyn Paperbacks Cash Sales, PO Box 11, Falmouth, Cornwall TR10 9EN

Please enclose remittance to the value of the cover price plus:

UK: 22p for the first book plus 10p per copy for each additional book ordered to a maximum charge of 92p.

BFPO and EIRE: 22p for the first book plus 10p per copy for the next 6 books, thereafter 4p per book.

OVERSEAS: 30p for the first book and 10p for each additional book.

Whilst every effort is made to keep prices low it is sometimes necessary to increase cover prices and also postage and packing rates at short notice. Hamlyn Paperbacks reserve the right to show new retail prices on covers which may differ from those previously advertised in the text or elsewhere.